The Pug Who Bit Napoleon

For John, a symbol of the best and fairest section of my life.

The Pug Who Bit Napoleon

Animal Tales of the 18th and 19th Centuries

Mimi Matthews

PEN & SWORD
HISTORY

First published in Great Britain in 2017 by
Pen & Sword History
an imprint of
Pen & Sword Books Ltd
47 Church Street
Barnsley
South Yorkshire
S70 2AS

ISBN 978 1 52670 500 6

A CIP catalogue record for this book is available from the British
Library.

Typeset in Ehrhardt by
Mac Style Ltd, Bridlington, East Yorkshire
Printed and bound in India by Replika Press Pvt. Ltd.

Pen & Sword Books Limited incorporates the imprints of Atlas,
Archaeology, Aviation, Discovery, Family History, Fiction, History,
Maritime, Military, Military Classics, Politics, Select, Transport,
True Crime, Air World, Frontline Publishing, Leo Cooper,
Remember When, Seaforth Publishing, The Praetorian Press,
Wharncliffe Local History, Wharncliffe Transport,
Wharncliffe True Crime and White Owl.

For a complete list of Pen & Sword titles please contact
PEN & SWORD BOOKS LIMITED
47 Church Street, Barnsley, South Yorkshire, S70 2AS, England
E-mail: enquiries@pen-and-sword.co.uk
Website: www.pen-and-sword.co.uk

Contents

Acknowledgments

Researching and writing is often a solitary endeavour; however, along the road from first draft to publication, I have been privileged to have an extraordinary amount of support and encouragement from friends, family, and professional peers. To them, I extend my heartfelt thanks.

Thanks are also due to the fabulous team at Pen and Sword Books; to commissioning editor Jon Wright who thought a book of historical animal tales was a great idea; to copy editor Carol Trow who handled my book with so much sensitivity and care; to production assistant Lauren Burton who patiently answered my endless e-mail questions; to designer Dominic Allen who created such a beautiful book jacket; and to fellow Pen and Sword author Sarah Murden who offered her moral support early in the process.

A very special thank you to the countless museums, universities, and archives that assisted in my research. I am particularly grateful to the British Library, the British Newspaper Archive, Yale University's Lewis Walpole Library, the Yale Center for British Art, Bryn Mawr College Library, the Pennsylvania Academy of Fine Arts, the National Galleries of Scotland, the Brontë Parsonage Museum in West Yorkshire, and the lovely people managing Lord Byron's collection at Newstead Abbey in Nottinghamshire.

I must also acknowledge the contribution of my own pets to this project, both those that are still living and those that have long since passed away. My dog, Ascher, and my two cats, Sapphire and Marzipan, were often beside me, lending their support while I researched and wrote. Orson, Ava, Sequin, Cleopatra, Jude, and my beloved John were also there in spirit. As for my horse, Centelleo, though he was not actually at my side as I worked, he was often in my thoughts, especially when writing my chapter on Whistlejacket.

Last, but certainly not least, I would like to thank my parents. To my wonderful mother, Vickie, thank you for raising me to love and respect all living creatures. Your sense of justice, fairness, and compassion has been the blueprint of my life. And to my amazing father, Eugene, thank you for always being in my corner. No girl could ask for a better dad.

Mimi Matthews
February 2017

Introduction

For centuries, humans have enjoyed a unique relationship with animals. Dogs have protected our flocks and guarded our shops, horses and donkeys have pulled our carts and carriages and cats have kept our homes and businesses free of vermin. But animals in eighteenth and nineteenth century history were much more than mere partners in the toils of daily life. They were companions and friends, beloved members of the family with unique lives and distinct personalities of their own. They were also a source of endless fascination and amusement to the public.

Tales of heroic dogs, intrepid cats, valiant horses and clever parrots and monkeys appeared with regularity in eighteenth and nineteenth century books, magazines, letters, journals and newspaper reports. Some of these tales were humorous, providing as much entertainment as a modern-day animal GIF or a meme. Some of these tales were horrifying, prompting concerned citizens to take action on behalf of the animal who had been mistreated or neglected. Most of all, however, animal tales of the eighteenth and nineteenth centuries were heart-warming, inspiring and relatable.

Love of animals crossed all social and cultural boundaries. Kings and Queens had their favourites, just as did those of more humble origins. These favourites were honoured in poems, paintings and popular novels. They also merited frequent mentions in letters written by literary luminaries such as Horace Walpole, Lord Byron and Charles Dickens, as well as in correspondence between eighteenth and nineteenth century royalty. Animals of every variety inspired art and literature, they figured into major historical events and stood at the side of some of the most influential human beings in history.

Animals of the eighteenth and nineteenth centuries also featured regularly in court cases and in the news. Some of these animals, like the bloodhounds hired to hunt Jack the Ripper, were more notable for their specific skills than for the particular bond they had with their masters. Others, like the killer shark caught in the Thames in 1787, came to public attention purely on account of the strange circumstances of their presence.

The unique stories of each of these animals are the primary focus of this book. In researching their histories, I have utilized a wide range of eighteenth and nineteenth century resources to verify the authenticity of each animal's tale. It has always been my personal belief that the closer in time one can get to the actual source, the more accurate the story. As a consequence, the majority of this book employs quotes from actual letters, journals, magazine articles and newspaper reports, as opposed to modern day, paraphrased variations of the same.

Many of the animals which I profile were depicted in famous paintings or drawn by their equally famous masters. In every instance, I have included the relevant piece of artwork. In addition, I have supplemented notable animal artwork throughout, including the work of eighteenth century animal painter George Stubbs and nineteenth century animal painter Edwin Henry Landseer. The animal paintings of Thomas Gainsborough, John Ferneley, Henriette Ronner-Knip, Rosa Bonheur and other distinguished artists of the eighteenth and nineteenth centuries are also well represented.

The animal tales I have chosen to highlight are by no means the only animal tales in history. Animal stories were not confined to a specific set of centuries, nor were they strictly limited to western culture. In the end, the stories I have researched and written on are stories that interest me personally. I hope you will find them as enjoyable to read as I have to write.

Pugs were fashionable companion dogs for ladies of wealth and rank throughout the eighteenth and nineteenth centuries. (*Princess Ekaterina Dmitrievna Golitsyna by Louis Michael van Loo, 1759 in the Pushkin Museum, Moscow. Bridgeman Images*)

Part I

Dogs

Chapter One

The Pug Who Bit Napoleon

'About thirty years ago, the fashionable lapdog was the Dutch-Pug; every old Duchess in the kingdom had three or four, and these ugly little animals were the ladies' favourites from the accession of William the Third to the death of George the Second.'

The *Sporting Magazine*, 1803

In the late eighteenth century, Joséphine de Beauharnais had a beloved lapdog named Fortune. He had been given to her as a young pup by her great friend Thérésa Cabarrus, Madame Tallien, and has been described as having a fawn or russet-coloured body, a black muzzle, and a curly tail. He was, in short, a pug – a breed of dog which had been quite fashionable for many years with society grand dames and aristocratic ladies of leisure. He was not the best example of his breed, either in appearance or temperament, but Joséphine would soon come to prize him above all of her other pets.

On 21 April 1794, at the height of the Reign of Terror, Joséphine was denounced as an enemy of the republic. She was arrested and taken away to be imprisoned in the Convent of the Carmelites. *Les Carmes* was a dank and sinister place, infested with vermin, and filled with prisoners who were sometimes forced to sleep as many as eighteen to a cell. Joséphine spent much of her time there playing solitaire and weeping.

Even so, the situation was not wholly intolerable. Joséphine's husband, Alexandre de Beauharnais was also imprisoned in *Les Carmes* and she was able to see him quite often. In addition, Joséphine was allowed regular visits from her children, Eugene and Hortense, and their governess, Madame Lanoy. These visits took place through the prison bars and in the presence of the turnkey. Intimate conversation was impossible. Luckily, Fortune was also allowed to visit the prison and, unlike Joséphine's children, he was able to slip through the bars and into his mistress's cell.

Fortune had been pining dreadfully in Joséphine's absence and, upon arriving at the prison with Eugene and Hortense, he would rush straight into Joséphine's waiting arms. These moments of affection between the future empress and her little pug facilitated a secret communication, for hidden beneath Fortune's collar were private messages from Joséphine's children and her friends. Joséphine

A portrait of a fawn–coloured Pug, similar to Fortune. (*Conradijn Cunaeus (Dutch, 1828–1895), Portrait of Pug Edwin vom Rath, 1880–1895. Pencil and watercolour. Rijksmuseum, Amsterdam. Bequest of Mr. JWE vom Rath*)

would stealthily remove these hidden notes and replace them with secret letters of her own. By this means, she was able to communicate with not only her family, but with influential friends who, she hoped, would help in securing her freedom, as well as the freedom of her husband.

Three months later, Joséphine was released from prison. Her husband, Alexandre, was not so fortunate. On 23 July 1794, he was guillotined at the Place de la Révolution. This left Joséphine a widow, paving the way for her marriage to Napoleon Bonaparte only two years later.

Fortune's role in carrying messages for his mistress while she was imprisoned during the Reign of Terror forever endeared him to both Joséphine and her children. As the little pug grew older, becoming even more bad-tempered as he aged, they were willing to forgive his many shortcomings, choosing instead to spoil him with caresses and praise. By 1796, Fortune's place in the hierarchy of the household – and in his mistress's affections – was unassailable. This fact did not bode well for her new husband.

Napoleon Bonaparte and Joséphine de Beauharnais were married on 9 March 1796. Napoleon was only twenty-six years old and it was his first marriage. Joséphine was a widow and six years his senior. Upon joining her in bed that evening, Napoleon was surprised to learn that the two newlyweds were not to be alone. Fortune was long accustomed to sleeping in his mistress's bed and no exception had been made for her wedding night. When Napoleon sought to have the dog removed, Joséphine stringently objected, insisting that Fortune remain not just in the bedroom, but in the marital bed.

Josephine as she appeared when crowned Empress of the French. (Jean-Baptiste Regnault (*French, 1754–1829), Empress Joséphine of France, n.d. Oil on canvas. Nationalmuseum, Stockholm*)

A portrait of a much older Napoleon, painted in his study at the Tuilleries, sixteen years after his wedding night encounter with Fortune. (*Jacques-Louis David (French, 1748–1825), The Emperor Napoleon in His Study at the Tuileries, 1812. Oil on canvas. Courtesy National Gallery of Art, Washington*)

Fortune was, by this point, well-known for his quarrelsome and aggressive behaviour. He had a reputation for snarling, snapping and biting the ankles of any stranger who dared approach his mistress in a threatening manner. Apparently, Fortune still considered Napoleon to be a stranger, for as the consummation commenced the little pug began to bark furiously. Napoleon made several attempts to cajole him. When that failed, the impatient bridegroom kicked Fortune from the bed.

Fortune was not so easily routed. He leapt back onto the bed and – as Napoleon resumed his marital duty – the livid little lapdog viciously bit him on the calf. Though not fatal, the wound inflicted by Fortune's teeth was really quite severe. As a result, the remainder of the wedding night was reportedly spent with Joséphine applying compresses to Napoleon's calf and Napoleon moaning that he 'was dying of hydrophobia'.[1]

Ultimately, Napoleon did not contract hydrophobia (or rabies as we know it today); however, Fortune's bad behaviour on his wedding night was neither forgiven nor forgotten. Napoleon would bear the scars from his diminutive rival's vicious assault for the rest of his life, a fact which he is known to have reflected on with some bitterness. On one occasion, for example, when talking to playwright Antoine-Vincent Arnault, Napoleon pointed at Fortune as the little pug lay on the sofa beside Joséphine and said:

> 'Do you see that gentleman? He is my rival. He was in possession of Madame's bed when I married her. I wished to remove him; it was quite useless to think of it. I was told that I must either sleep elsewhere, or consent to share my bed. That annoyed me considerably, but I had to make up my mind. I gave way. The favourite was less accommodating; I bear proofs on my leg of what I say.'[2]

Despite his own feelings, Napoleon was well aware of the deep affection that Joséphine had for her pug. He mentions Fortune in several of his subsequent love letters to Joséphine, closing one sent on 17 July 1796 – a mere four months after their disastrous wedding night – with the following sentiment, 'Millions of kisses, some even to Fortune, in spite of his naughtiness.'

In another letter, Napoleon loses his temper with his new bride when, after months of begging her to leave Paris and join him on campaign in Italy, she has still not arrived. Jealous and frustrated, he writes:

> 'You ought to have started on May 24th. Being good-natured, I waited till June 1st, as if a pretty woman would give up her habits, her friends, both Madame Tallien and a dinner with Barras, and the acting of a new play, and Fortune; yes, Fortune, whom you love much more than your husband, for whom you have only a little of the esteem, and a share of that benevolence with which your heart abounds!'[3]

After nearly four months of excuses, Joséphine finally consented to join Napoleon in Italy. She did not make the journey alone. With her in a three carriage convoy, complete with a full accompaniment of luggage, servants, and a cavalry escort, was her brother-in-law, Joseph Bonaparte; her new husband's aide-de-camp, Colonel Junot; her current lover, Hippolyte Charles; and her pug, Fortune.

In Italy, Fortune became a fast favourite. According to an 1842 edition of the *Court Magazine and Monthly Critic*, he was 'caressed and petted by all the officers on the staff' and soon regarded as 'an important personage at headquarters'. Napoleon himself was less than pleased. Time and distance had not improved his opinion of the pampered pug. He tolerated him for Joséphine's sake only. But he would not have to tolerate him for much longer. Fortune was destined to meet his end in a most unfortunate way.

One day, while roaming the gardens at Montebello, Fortune encountered the cook's giant dog. In some historical accounts this dog is described as a mastiff and in others a bulldog. Whatever he was, he did not take kindly to Fortune's threatening snaps and snarls. When Fortune attempted to assert his dominance, the cook's dog seized the little pug in his jaws, breaking his ribs in one bite. Within a few hours, Fortune was dead.

Napoleon was far from grief-stricken by this turn of events and he had no patience with anyone who was. When he found one of the guards on duty inside the palace weeping over Fortune's demise, the *Court Magazine and Monthly Critic* reports that he had the soldier put under twenty-four-hour arrest, telling him, 'Deep rooted griefs require quiet and solitude.'

Joséphine's own grief was not so easily managed. Devastated by the loss of Fortune, she was utterly inconsolable. Napoleon forbade her from acquiring another pug, but Hippolyte Charles, unable to bear the sight of his lover's tears, lost no time in presenting her with a pug puppy.

Sometime later, Napoleon crossed paths with the cook. The remorseful servant apologized for his dog killing Fortune and assured Napoleon that the larger dog had been sent away never to return. Napoleon allegedly replied, 'Bring him back. Perhaps he will rid me of the new one too!'[4]

Pugs would continue to be popular companion dogs throughout the Victorian era. (*James Tissot (French, 1836–1902), Young Woman in a Boat, or Reflections, 1870. Oil on canvas. Private Collection/Bridgeman Images*)

Wealthy ladies and gentlemen of the eighteenth and nineteenth centuries often commissioned portraits of their favourite dogs from prominent painters of the era. (*Thomas Gainsborough RA (British, 1727–1788), Spitz Dog, 1765. Oil on canvas. Yale Center for British Art, Paul Mellon Collection*)

In addition to horses, famed eighteenth century equine artist George Stubbs also painted dogs and other animals. (*George Stubbs (British, 1724–1806), Brown and White Norfolk or Water Spaniel, 1778. Oil on panel. Yale Center for British Art, Paul Mellon Collection*)

Chapter Two

The Devoted Great Dane of Alexander Pope

'Histories are more full of examples of the fidelity of dogs than of friends.'
Alexander Pope, 1709

Eighteenth century poet and satirist Alexander Pope was a lover of dogs all of his life. He preferred large dogs as his writing occasionally provoked threats of violence from those he attacked with his acerbic wit. Small, frail and stricken at a young age with a form of tuberculosis that affected his spine, he was incapable of defending himself in an actual physical altercation and depended on his canine guardians to protect him.

Over the years, Pope owned a succession of Great Danes, each by the name of Bounce. The first Bounce was a male dog, as was the last. The rest were all females, the most well-known of which was the 'great faithful Danish dog' that Pope owned in 1728.[5] Following publication of the *Dunciad*, Pope received a great many threats. On one occasion, he is even rumoured to have been beaten by two gentlemen who set upon him during one of his walks. Such a traumatic experience made him extraordinarily cautious about his safety and, in future, he never went out walking unless he was accompanied by Bounce – and a pair of pistols.

Pope was a small man, standing no more than four and a half feet tall. Bounce was of an equal height. Any other dog so large might have overpowered such a diminutive master, but Bounce was generally well-mannered. The only time she posed any danger to Pope was when she was released from a prolonged period of confinement. It was then that, in her exuberance, she sometimes knocked Pope down. George Lyttleton alludes to this in a letter sent to Pope on 22 December 1736 in which he writes:

'You need not be told that the desire of seeing you is one great cause of that impatience; but to show you how much I am master of my passions, I will be quiet here for a week or ten days longer, and then come to you in most outrageous spirits, and overturn you like Bounce, when you let her loose after a regimen of physic and confinement.'

A portrait of Alexander Pope with one of the many incarnations of Great Danes named Bounce. (*Jonathan Richardson (British, 1665–1745), Alexander Pope and His Dog, Bounce, 1718. Oil on canvas. Private Collection / Bridgeman Images*)

Alexander Pope at the age of fifty. (Jonathan Richardson (*British, 1665–1745*), *Alexander Pope, 1738. Oil on canvas. Yale Center for British Art, Paul Mellon Collection*)

When Bounce wasn't overturning Pope, she was protecting him and lending him her support as he wrote. While Pope worked, she lay quietly at his feet. While Pope entertained, she socialized with the guests and happily received their every attention. She even inspired a poem or two, the most famous of which was the 1736 poem titled *Bounce to Fop: An Heroic Epistle from a Dog at Twickenham to a Dog at Court*. Written as if Bounce is addressing a spaniel named Fop, it is a satire of courtiers and court life.

BOUNCE TO FOP

To thee, sweet Fop, these Lines I send,
Who, tho' no Spaniel, am a Friend.
Tho, once my Tail in wanton play,
Now frisking this, and then that way,
Chanc'd, with a Touch of just the Tip,
To hurt your Lady-lap-dog-ship;
Yet thence to think I'd bite your Head off!
Sure Bounce is one you never read of.

FOP! you can dance, and make a Leg,
Can fetch and carry, cringe and beg,
And (what's the Top of all your Tricks)
Can stoop to pick up Strings and Sticks.
We Country Dogs love nobler Sport,
And scorn the Pranks of Dogs at Court.
Fye, naughty Fop! where e'er you come
To f – t and p – ss about the Room,
To lay your Head in every Lap,
And, when they think not of you – snap!
The worst that Envy, or that Spite
E'er said of me, is, I can bite:
That sturdy Vagrants, Rogues in Rags,
Who poke at me, can make no Brags;
And that to towze such Things as flutter,
To honest Bounce is Bread and Butter.
While you, and every courtly Fop,
Fawn on the Devil for a Chop,
I've the Humanity to hate
A Butcher, tho' he brings me Meat;
And let me tell you, have a Nose,
(Whatever stinking Fops suppose)
That under Cloth of Gold or Tissue,
Can smell a Plaister, or an Issue.

Your pilf'ring Lord, with simple Pride,
May wear a Pick-lock at his Side;
My Master wants no Key of State,
For Bounce can keep his House and Gate.

When all such Dogs have had their Days,
As knavish Pams, and fawning Trays;
When pamper'd Cupids, bestly Veni's,
And motly, squinting Harvequini's,
Shall lick no more their Lady's Br – ,
But die of Looseness, Claps, or Itch;
Fair Thames from either ecchoing Shoare
Shall hear, and dread my manly Roar.

See Bounce, like Berecynthia, crown'd
With thund'ring Offspring all around,
Beneath, beside me, and a top,
A hundred Sons! and not one Fop.

Before my Children set your Beef,
Not one true Bounce will be a Thief;
Not one without Permission feed,
(Tho' some of J – 's hungry Breed)
But whatsoe'er the Father's Race,
From me they suck a little Grace.
While your fine Whelps learn all to steal,
Bred up by Hand on Chick and Veal.

My Eldest-born resides not far,
Where shines great Strafford's glittering Star:
My second (Child of Fortune!) waits
At Burlington's Palladian Gates:
A third majestically stalks
(Happiest of Dogs!) in Cobham's Walks:
One ushers Friends to Bathurst's Door;
One fawns, at Oxford's, on the Poor.

Nobles, whom Arms or Arts adorn,
Wait for my Infants yet unborn.
None but a Peer of Wit and Grace,
Can hope a Puppy of my Race.

And O! wou'd Fate the Bliss decree
To mine (a Bliss too great for me)
That two, my tallest Sons, might grace
Attending each with stately Pace,
Iulus' Side, as erst Evander's,

To keep off Flatt'rers, Spies, and Panders,
To let no noble Slave come near,
And scare Lord Fannys from his Ear:
Then might a Royal Youth, and true,
Enjoy at least a Friend – or two:
A Treasure, which, of Royal kind,
Few but Himself deserve to find.

Then Bounce ('tis all that Bounce can crave)
Shall wag her Tail within the Grave.

And tho' no Doctors, Whig or Tory ones,
Except the Sect of Pythagoreans,
Have Immortality assign'd
To any Beast, but Dryden's Hind:
Yet Master Pope, whom Truth and Sense
Shall call their Friend some Ages hence,
Tho' now on loftier Themes he sings

Alexander Pope's Villa, Twickenham, where he lived with Bounce. (*Joseph Nickolls (British, active 1713–ca. 1755), Pope's Villa, Twickenham, ca. 1755. Oil on canvas. Yale Center for British Art, Paul Mellon Collection*)

Than to bestow a Word on Kings,
Has sworn by Sticks (the Poet's Oath,
And Dread of Dogs and Poets both)
Man and his Works he'll soon renounce,
And roar in Numbers worthy Bounce.

Bounce did have 'thund'ring Offspring all around'. As referenced in *Bounce to Fop*, puppies from a 1736 litter by Bounce found their way into the homes of the Earl of Strafford, the Earl of Burlington, Viscount Cobham, and Lord Bathurst. Perhaps the most celebrated puppy of all was the one given as a gift to Frederick, Prince of Wales. It came with a collar upon which had been engraved Pope's now legendary lines: 'I am His Highness' Dog at Kew; Pray tell me Sir, whose Dog are you?'

But Bounce was much more than a literary muse. One night, she actually saved Pope's life. Earlier that day, Pope had hired a new valet. Bounce took an instant dislike to the man and, that evening, after the valet helped Pope into bed, she crept into his chamber to keep watch over him while he slept.

Pope was later awakened by the sound of Bounce struggling to subdue an intruder that she had pinned to the ground by his throat. Pope hurried to the window to scream for help. His servants responded at once, quickly managing to capture three more thieves who had been lurking in the garden. As for the intruder apprehended by Bounce, he proved to be none other than Pope's own valet. Armed with a pistol, he had intended to murder Pope and rob the house with his confederates.

The last incarnation of Bounce was a male Great Dane. He died in 1744 after being bitten by a mad dog while in the care of John Boyle, 5th Earl of Orrery at Marston House, Somerset. Alexander Pope wrote to Lord Orrery after his death on the 10 April 1744. His letter reads, in part:

'I dread to enquire into the particulars of the Fate of Bounce. Perhaps you conceald them, as Heav'n often does Unhappy Events, in pity to the Survivors, or not to hasten on my End by Sorrow. I doubt not how much Bounce was lamented: They might say as the Athenians did to Arcite, in Chaucer,

"Ah Arcite! gentle Knight! Why would'st though die,
When though had'st Gold enough, and Emilye?
Ah Bounce! ah gentle Beast! why wouldst thou dye,
When thou hadst Meat enough and Orrery?"'

The above verse, which was published posthumously and is known now as *Lines on Bounce*, is generally acknowledged as the last that Alexander Pope ever wrote. He died less than two months later on the 30 May 1744. I cannot help but feel that the news of Bounce's death did, in fact, hasten on his end by sorrow.

Both companion dogs and hunting/sporting dogs were portrayed in eighteenth and nineteenth century animal portraits. (*George Stubbs (British, 1724–1806), White Poodle in a Punt, c. 1780. Oil on canvas. Courtesy National Gallery of Art, Washington*)

Many of the dog breeds depicted in eighteenth and nineteenth century animal paintings look very different from what those breeds look like today. (*James Ward (British, 1769–1859), Rough-Coated Collie, 1809. Oil on board. Yale Center for British Art, Paul Mellon Collection*)

Chapter Three

The Spaniel Willed to Horace Walpole

'My poor dear Madame du Deffand's little dog is arrived. She made me promise to take care of it the last time I saw her: that I will most religiously, and make it as happy as is possible.'

Letter from Horace Walpole, 4 May 1781

In the present day, it is not uncommon for people to make provisions for their surviving pets when writing out their wills. Many animal lovers in the eighteenth and nineteenth century were similarly inclined. For example, renowned beauty Frances Teresa Stuart, Duchess of Richmond, spent the final years of her life in seclusion with only her cats for company. When she died in 1702, her will stated that those cats still living were to be divided amongst several female friends, each with legacies for their support. This posthumous generosity to her feline companions is generally understood to be the inspiration for Alexander Pope's famous lines:

'But thousands die, without or this or that,
　Die and endow a college or a cat.'

Eighteenth century British statesman Philip Stanhope, 4th Earl of Chesterfield, was also an animal lover. When he died in 1773, he left life pensions to his cats and their offspring. John Scott, Earl of Eldon, Lord Chancellor of Great Britain from 1801 to 1806 and again from 1807 to 1827, was equally generous to his beloved dog, Pincher. Pincher had originally belonged to Lord Eldon's son, William Henry. When William Henry died in 1836, his last request was that his father 'take care of poor Pincher'.[6] As Eldon recounts in one of his letters:

'The dog was brought home to me when all was over: and in a short time he was missed. He was immediately sought for, and he was found lying on the bed beside his dead master. Poor Pincher! I would not lose him on any account.[7]

Pincher, a German spaniel, would become Lord Eldon's constant companion and, upon Eldon's death in 1838, he bequeathed to his daughter, Frances, an

Sir Edwin Henry Landseer was the preeminent animal painter of the nineteenth century. (*Sir Edwin Henry Landseer (British, 1802–1873), A Spaniel Lying Down, 1860. Oil on panel. Yale Center for British Art, Paul Mellon Collection*)

annual sum of £8 for Pincher's food and maintenance. Pincher would live on to be painted by renowned animal portraitist Edwin Henry Landseer, who called him 'a very picturesque old dog with a great look of cleverness in his face'.[8] He died at an advanced age in May of 1840 and was buried at the Eldon Seat at Encombe. An inscription there commemorates him as the Lord Chancellor's favourite dog.

The nobility were not the only figures of the eighteenth and nineteenth century to provide for their pets in their wills. According to an 1895 edition of *The Living Age*:

'A gentleman who died in 1805, at Knightsbridge, left a pension of £25 to four dogs, descendants of a faithful animal who saved his life when attacked by brigands while travelling in Italy.'

Another account tells of a wealthy London widow who bequeathed an annuity of £200 to a pet parrot that had been her faithful companion for nearly twenty-five years. A shrewd woman, who was no doubt well aware of the temptation a caregiver might have to abandon, or possibly kill, the bird and pocket the money, her will specified that the pet parrot must be produced twice a year or else all payments to the caregiver would cease.

And then there is the tale of a lady who died in 1828 leaving the sum of £10 to her pet monkey and £5 each to her cat and dog. Her will specified that if any one

The silver gilt over brass snuff box with wax portrait of Tonton which was willed to Horace Walpole upon the death of his dear friend, Madame du Deffand. (*Louis Roucel (French, d.1787) and Isaac Gosset (British, 1713–1799). Courtesy of The Lewis Walpole Library, Yale University*)

animal should die, the remaining money would be divided amongst the surviving pets. If all the pets died, the remaining funds were then to revert to her daughter.

By far my favourite tale – and certainly one worthy of attention all on its own – is of Tonton, the ill-tempered dog bequeathed to Horace Walpole, 4th Earl of Orford, by his close friend Marie Anne de Vichy-Chamrond, Marquise du Deffand, upon her death in 1780. Along with the dog, Madame du Deffand willed Walpole a stipend for Tonton's upkeep as well as a gilt snuffbox with Tonton's portrait on the lid.

Tonton was a famously vicious little spaniel, especially when in the presence of his mistress. In a letter to his cousin, Henry Seymour Conway, dated 8 September

1775, Walpole recounts an incident that occurred while Madame du Deffand was still alive:

> 'T'other night [Tonton] flew at Lady Barrymore's face, and I thought would have torn her eye out; but it ended in biting her finger. She was terrified; she fell into tears. Madame du Deffand, who has too much parts not to see everything in its true light, perceiving that she had not beaten Tonton half enough, immediately told us a story of a lady, whose dog having bitten a piece out of a gentleman's leg, the tender dame, in a great fright, cried out, "Won't it make my dog sick?"'

After the death of Madame du Deffand, Walpole took Tonton home with him. The initial period of adjustment was a difficult one. In a letter to Conway, dated 6 May 1781, he writes:

> 'I brought [Tonton] this morning to take possession of his new villa; but his inauguration has not been at all pacific. As he has already found out that he may be as despotic as at Saint Joseph's, he began with exiling my beautiful little cat; – upon which, however, we shall not quite agree. He then flew at one of my dogs, who returned it, by biting his foot till it bled.'

In time, Tonton did adjust – at least to Walpole, who grew to love the little dog enormously. Unfortunately, he was still aggressive with everyone else. Letters abound in which Walpole writes of Tonton's various misdemeanours. He bit people's fingers. He destroyed their furniture. Walpole was even obliged to equip him with a 'privy purse' whenever they travelled in order to bribe servants not to reveal the damage that Tonton had done to his host's furnishings. Walpole references this in a letter to Countess Ossory, dated 4 July 1781, in which he writes:

Portrait of a young Horace Walpole. (*Allan Ramsay (Scottish, 1713–1784), Portrait of Horace Walpole, c. 1759. Oil on canvas. Courtesy of The Lewis Walpole Library, Yale University*)

> 'Do not be afraid, you shall not be plagued with Tonton, though I assure you he has a very decent

Horace Walpole in his library at Strawberry Hill, Twickenham with one of his earlier pet dogs. (*Johann Heinrich Müntz (Swiss, 1727–1798), Portrait of Horace Walpole in his Library, 1755–1759. Drawing. Courtesy of The Lewis Walpole Library, Yale University*)

privy purse for his travels; but I recollect that my uncle Horace used to say that Mademoiselle Furniture does not love dogs; which makes me allow Tonton handsomely, that he may silence such tattling housekeepers as Margaret.'

Tonton would become the last of Horace Walpole's favourite dogs. In February 1789, he passed away at Walpole's side 'without a pang or a groan'. In a letter to the Countess Ossory, dated 24 February 1789, Walpole declared:

'I have had the satisfaction, for my dear old friend's sake and his own, of having nursed him up, by constant attention, to the age of sixteen, yet always afraid of his surviving me, as it was scarcely possible he could meet a third person who would study his happiness equally.'

Tonton was buried behind the chapel at Horace Walpole's Twickenham estate, Strawberry Hill. When asked by the Countess of Ossory if she could give him another dog to replace Tonton, Walpole declined. As he explained in his letter of 24 February:

'I shall miss [Tonton] greatly, and must not have another dog; I am too old, and should only breed it up to be unhappy, when I am gone.'

A portrait of Lord Byron's Newfoundland, Boatswain, painted the same year that Boatswain died. (*Clifton Thomson* (*British, 1775–1828*), *Portrait of Lord Byron's Dog Boatswain, 1808. Oil on canvas. By permission of Nottingham City Museums and Galleries*)

Chapter Four

Lord Byron's Firmest Friend

'Byron's fondness for dogs accompanied him throughout his life.'
Researches Into the History of the
British Dog George Jesse, 1866

Legendary nineteenth century romantic poet George Gordon Byron, 6th Baron Byron had a great fondness for animals. He kept a veritable menagerie of pets during his lifetime, including dogs, cats, horses, monkeys, several varieties of birds and, at one point, even a bear. From amongst all of these, his favourite, and by far his best known, was undoubtedly his dog, Boatswain.

Acquired when Byron was only fifteen, Boatswain is most often described as a Newfoundland. However, Boatswain did not look much like the Newfoundland breed we know today. A contemporary portrait shows that, instead of being solid black, he was black and white. And instead of being enormous and rather fluffy, he was lean and smooth-coated, built along the lines of a German shepherd or a Siberian husky. Nevertheless, Boatswain is said to have had all the instinctive abilities for which the Newfoundland breed was known – most significant of which was a propensity for water rescue.

One of Byron's favourite games to play with Boatswain was to simulate drowning in order to encourage Boatswain to dive into the water and rescue him. While staying at Newstead Abbey, Byron's ancestral home in Nottinghamshire, Byron would often row out onto the lake and, when he was sure Boatswain was watching, purposefully fall out of his boat and into the water. Boatswain would then plunge into the lake and drag Byron safely to the shore.

At the time that Byron owned Boatswain, he also owned a ferocious bullmastiff named Nelson. Nelson and Boatswain were mortal enemies. Byron generally kept Nelson muzzled, but on those rare occasions he was free of constraint, Nelson would go straight for Boatswain's throat. During the summer of 1806, the fights between the two dogs were particularly vicious. Byron's friend and fellow poet Thomas Moore was vacationing with him that summer at Harrowgate and had an opportunity to witness these canine battles first hand. He writes:

'There was always a jealous feud between this Nelson and Boatswain, and whenever the latter came into the room while the former was there, they

An 1856 engraving which depicts
Lord Byron in his prime. (*Lord
Byron*, 1856. Engraving on steel)

instantly seized each other, and then Byron, myself, Frank, and all the waiters
that could be found, were vigorously engaged in parting them; which was, in
general, only effected by thrusting poker and tongs into the mouth of each.'

Nelson was not the only dog with whom Boatswain had a rivalry. Lord Byron's
mother, Lady Byron, had a little fox terrier named Gilpin with whom Boatswain
was 'perpetually at war'. Boatswain took every opportunity to attack Gilpin and
many in the family worried he would eventually kill the much smaller dog. As a
result, when Byron left for Cambridge, Mrs. Byron sent Gilpin away to live with
a tenant at Newstead Abbey.

Boatswain was unsettled by the loss of his rival. One morning, he simply
disappeared. The servant to whom Byron had entrusted Boatswain while he was
away at school fell into a panic. He looked for Boatswain high and low, but could
find him nowhere. Finally, at dusk, Boatswain reappeared. He was not alone.
With him was Gilpin. Boatswain led the little terrier straight to the kitchen fire
where he licked him and lavished upon him 'every possible demonstration of
joy'. As Moore reports:

'The fact was, he had been all the way to Newstead to fetch him, and
having now established his former foe under the roof once more, agreed so
perfectly well with him ever after, that he even protected him against the

insults of other dogs (a task which the quarrelsomeness of the little terrier rendered no sinecure); and if he but heard Gilpin's voice in distress, would fly instantly to his rescue.'

As demonstrated by his daylong excursion to retrieve Gilpin, Boatswain had considerable freedom in the country. It was his regular habit to follow the post boy into the nearby town of Mansfield. In November of 1808, during one of these excursions, Boatswain was bitten by a rabid dog. Initially, Byron was unaware that his pet had contracted rabies. Seeing only that Boatswain was terribly ill, Byron remained by his side until the end, sometimes even going so far as to wipe Boatswain's foaming mouth with his bare hand.

Boatswain died on 18 November 1808. Byron was inconsolable. That same day, he wrote to his friend, Reverend Francis Hodgson, announcing the death in anguished tones:

'Boatswain is dead! – he expired in a state of madness on the 18th after suffering much, yet retaining all the gentleness of his nature to the last, never attempting to do the least injury to any one near him. I have now lost everything except old Murray.'

Newstead Abbey in Nottinghamshire, the home of Lord Byron and Boatswain. (*Louis Haghe (1806–1885) after Moses Webster (1792–1870), Newstead Abbey, The Seat of the Late Lord Byron, undated. Lithograph on moderately thick, slightly textured, cream wove paper. Yale Center for British Art, Paul Mellon Collection*)

In another letter, addressed to Hodgson on 27 November 1808, Byron expresses his wish to be buried with his deceased pet, writing:

'Boatswain is to be buried in a vault waiting for myself. I have also written an epitaph, which I would send, were it not for two reasons: one is, that it is too long for a letter; and the other, that I hope you will some day read it on the spot where it will be engraved.'

Boatswain was buried in the gardens of Newstead Abbey. Inscribed on his tomb is the epitaph that Byron referenced in his 1808 letter to Hodgson. The opening lines were contributed by Byron's friend, John Hobhouse, but the remainder of the poem was composed by Lord Byron himself. It reads:

EPITAPH TO A DOG

Near this Spot
are deposited the Remains of one
who possessed Beauty without Vanity,
Strength without Insolence,
Courage without Ferocity,
and all the virtues of Man without his Vices.

This praise, which would be unmeaning Flattery
if inscribed over human Ashes,
is but a just tribute to the Memory of
Boatswain, a Dog,
who was born in Newfoundland May 1803
and died at Newstead Nov. 18th, 1808.

When some proud Son of Man returns to Earth,
Unknown to Glory, but upheld by Birth,
The sculptor's art exhausts the pomp of woe,
And storied urns record who rests below.
When all is done, upon the Tomb is seen
Not what he was, but what he should have been.
But the poor Dog, in life the firmest friend,
The first to welcome, foremost to defend,
Whose honest heart is still his Master's own,
Who labours, fights, lives, breathes for him alone,
Unhonoured falls, unnoticed all his worth,
Denied in heaven the Soul he held on earth;

While man, vain insect! hopes to be forgiven,
And claims himself a sole exclusive heaven.
Oh man! thou feeble tenant of an hour,
Debased by slavery, or corrupt by power,
Who knows thee well, must quit thee with disgust,
Degraded mass of animated dust!
Thy love is lust, thy friendship all a cheat,
Thy tongue hypocrisy, thy heart deceit!
By nature vile, ennobled but by name,
Each kindred brute might bid thee blush for shame.
Ye, who behold perchance this simple urn,
Pass on – it honours none you wish to mourn.
To mark a friend's remains these stones arise;
I never knew but one – and here he lies.

Time did not dull Byron's grief. Nor did he forget his desire to be buried beside his beloved dog. In a rough draft of his will sent to his attorney on 12 August 1811, he even went so far as to include the following provision:

'The body of Lord B. to be buried in the vault of the garden of Newstead, without any ceremony or burial-service whatever, or any inscription, save his name and age. His dog not to be removed from the said vault.'

Byron's final wish would not come to pass. He died at Missolonghi in Western Greece on 19 April 1824 while fighting in the Greek War of Independence. By

that time, Newstead Abbey had been sold. When Byron's remains were returned to England, instead of being entombed with Boatswain, he was interred alongside his mother at the Byron family church in Hucknall, Nottinghamshire. Today, Boatswain's memorial at Newstead Abbey still stands as a lasting testament to the love of one of the world's greatest poets for his faithful canine friend.

An illustration of Boatswain's monument at Newstead Abbey. (*H. A. Powell, "Boatswain's Grave," 1936. By permission of Nottingham City Museums and Galleries*)

A portrait of a Dandie Dinmont Terrier by English equine artist John Ferneley who was famous for his paintings of horses and hunting scenes. (*John Ferneley (British, 1782–1860), A Dandie Dinmont Terrier, 1848. Oil on canvas. Yale Center for British Art, Paul Mellon Collection*)

Greyhounds have long been associated with wealth, privilege, and royalty. (*Charles Hancock (British, 1802–1877), Two Greyhounds in a Landscape, between 1830 and 1850. Oil on canvas. Yale Center for British Art, Paul Mellon Collection*)

Chapter Five

Prince Albert's Favourite Greyhound

'She was my companion from my fourteenth to my twenty-fifth year, a symbol therefore of the best and fairest section of my life.'
Letter from Prince Albert, 31 July 1844

Queen Victoria and Prince Albert were two of the most influential animal lovers of the nineteenth century. They were especially fond of dogs and whether at Buckingham Palace, Balmoral Castle, or Osborne House, they were rarely without their faithful pack of assorted terriers, hounds, collies, pugs and spaniels. Eos the Greyhound, however, belonged to Prince Albert alone. Given to him as a six-week-old puppy when he was a boy of only fourteen, Eos grew into a sleek, elegant dog with a jet black coat, a white streak on her nose, and four white feet. Albert raised and trained her himself and she became the constant companion of his youth.

At the age of twenty, when Albert sailed to England to marry Queen Victoria, Eos came with him from Germany. She was wholly devoted to the prince, following him everywhere, sitting at his feet during meals and even eating morsels of food from his fork. Albert was no less devoted to Eos. He recorded every event in her life in his journal, no matter how trivial. He also frequently mentioned her in the letters he exchanged with Victoria and other of his many royal relations around the world.

When the Princess Royal was born in 1840, Queen Victoria commissioned Britain's foremost animal painter, Sir Edwin Henry Landseer, to paint a portrait of Eos with the new baby for Prince Albert's birthday. Eos would go on to feature in several other Landseer paintings, both alone and with Prince Albert and the royal children. Other Victorian animal artists painted Eos as well, including George Morley who, in 1841, produced an oil on canvas which depicted Eos alongside her adult pups, Timur and Mishka. Eos was also the frequent subject of etchings and pencil sketches by Queen Victoria herself.

In January 1841, Eos was accidentally shot by Prince Ferdinand, Queen Victoria's Uncle. Victoria shared the news with another of her uncles, Leopold, King of the Belgians, in a letter dated 1 February 1842, writing:

'You have heard our great misfortune about dear Eos; she is going on well, but slowly, and still makes us rather anxious. It made me quite ill the first day, and keeps me fidgety still, till we know that she is quite safe.'

Queen Victoria commissioned this painting of Eos from animal painter Sir Edwin Henry Landseer as a Christmas present for Prince Albert in 1841 (*Sir Edwin Henry Landseer (British, 1802–1873), Eos, 1841. Oil on canvas. Royal Collection Trust ©Her Majesty Queen Elizabeth II, 2016/Bridgeman Images*)

An aquatint engraving of His Royal Highness Prince Albert. (*after George Baxter (British, 1804–1867), Prince Albert, after 1855. Aquatint, stipple engraving, etching and color woodcut on moderately thick, smooth, cream wove paper. Yale Center for British Art, Paul Mellon Collection*)

Leopold's prompt reply, dated 4 February 1842, reveals just how well thought of Eos was by the royal family. The letter reads in part:

'I was extremely sorry to hear the accident which befell dear Eos, a great friend of mine. I do not understand how your uncle managed it; he ought rather to have shot somebody else of the family.'

The royal family were not the only ones distressed by Eos's injury. Former prime minister William Lamb, 2nd Viscount Melbourne, was also troubled by the news that Eos had been hurt. He sent a letter to Queen Victoria on 1 February 1842, writing:

'Lord Melbourne was in despair at hearing of poor Eos. Favourites often get shot; Lord Melbourne has known it happen often in his time. That is the worst of dogs; they add another strong interest to a life which has already of itself interest enough, and those, God knows! Sufficiently subject both to accident and decay.'

Eos slowly recovered from her injuries and, on 8 February 1842, Queen Victoria wrote to her Uncle Leopold again, informing him that Eos was 'quite convalescent' and was presently walking about 'wrapped up in a flannel.' By the following autumn, Eos was well enough to go coursing with Victoria and Albert's other sighthounds. According to Victoria, Eos ran and fetched pheasants from great distances and 'coursed better than all the other young dogs.'

The following year, Eos had another health scare, albeit a minor one. In a letter to her Uncle Leopold, dated 28 March 1843, Victoria makes reference to a 'sudden attack' that Eos has suffered. Victoria attributed this attack to overeating, confessing to her uncle that Eos 'steals whenever she can get anything'. She also blamed the fact that Eos lived in rooms that were too warm and took too little exercise. Her remedy for this, as she wrote to her uncle, was that Eos 'must be well starved, poor thing, and not allowed to sleep in beds, as she generally does'.

On the morning of 31 July 1844, Eos was found dead at Windsor Castle. Prince Albert was deeply grieved by her loss. He sent a letter to his grandmother the very next day, writing:

'I am sure you will share my sorrow at this loss. She was a singularly clever creature, and had been for eleven years faithfully devoted to me. How many recollections are linked with her! She was my companion from my fourteenth to my twenty-fifth year, a symbol therefore of the best and fairest section of my life.'

Eos was buried on the Slopes at Windsor, her grave marked by a bronze model of a greyhound cast in her own likeness. Her monument, along with those of many other of Victoria and Albert's treasured pets, can still be found there today.

The eight-month-old Victoria, Princess Royal is portrayed with Eos in this 1841 Landseer painting which was commissioned by Queen Victoria for Prince Albert's birthday. (*Sir Edwin Henry Landseer (British, 1802–1873), Victoria, Princess Royal, with Eos, 1841. Oil on canvas. Royal Collection Trust ©Her Majesty Queen Elizabeth II, 2016/Bridgeman Images*)

A group portrait of some of the royal pets, including Hector the Scottish deerhound, Nero the Greyhound, Queen Victoria's spaniel Dash, and her parrot, Lory. (*Sir Edwin Henry Landseer (British, 1802–1873), Hector, Nero and Dash with the parrot, Lory, 1838. Oil on canvas. Royal Collection Trust ©Her Majesty Queen Elizabeth II, 2016/Bridgeman Images*)

Chapter Six

Emily Brontë and Her Dog Keeper

'To walk with her bulldog, Keeper, over the moors is her best adventure.'
Emily Brontë Agnes Mary Frances Robinson, 1883

During their short lives at Haworth Parsonage in West Yorkshire, the Brontë sisters kept a wide variety of household pets. Dogs, cats and even canaries feature heavily in their letters and journals, with the death of each duly mourned and remarked upon. Amongst these many animals (each of which I have no doubt deserves a story of their own), perhaps none is so well known to history as Emily Brontë's bulldog, Keeper.

In her 1857 biography of Emily's sister, Charlotte, Victorian author Elizabeth Gaskell describes Keeper as 'a tawny bull-dog'. He had been given to Emily as a gift, along with the warning that, though he was 'faithful to the depths of his nature' when among friends, he would viciously attack anyone who dared strike him with a stick or a whip.[9] This propensity for aggression did not frighten Emily; quite the opposite in fact. Keeper soon became her favourite pet and constant companion. She loved nothing better than walking with him on the moors or sitting with him on the hearthrug in the parlour, one arm 'thrown round' his neck as she read a book.[10]

Keeper featured in Emily's literary life as well. When she was revealed as the author of *Wuthering Heights*, many puzzled over how an isolated clergyman's daughter could have imagined such a dark and passionate tale. Attempting to solve the mystery, an article in the 1857 issue of *Littell's Living Age* refers to Keeper as Emily's familiar, using her affinity with him and other animals to explain why *Wuthering Heights* was populated with 'instinctive, soulless, savage' characters, more resembling a pack of hounds than respectable human beings. As *Littell's* rationalizes:

'Here her sympathy with animals, and utter want of sympathy with human nature, together with certain animal qualities in herself, as for instance, a dogged temper, supply a solution to what would otherwise be an impenetrable mystery – how a quiet, reserved, as far as we are informed, steady and well-conducted young woman, a clergyman's daughter, living all her life in a remote parsonage, and seeing nobody, could have conceived such scenes, or couched her conceptions in such language.'

Emily's bond with Keeper was, indeed, a close one. She was devoted to him, feeding him from her own hands and teaching him various tricks. According to an 1871 edition of *Scribner's Monthly Magazine*:

> 'He was so completely under her control, she could quite easily make him spring and roar like a lion. She taught him this kind of occasional play without any coercion.'

Despite his close relationship with Emily, Keeper had one 'household fault'.[11] He loved nothing better than sneaking upstairs, leaping up onto one of the beds, and stretching out on the clean, white counterpane. Those in the Brontë household found this unhygienic canine habit to be wholly objectionable, with Emily herself declaring that:

> 'If he was found again transgressing, she herself, in defiance of warning and his well-known ferocity of nature, would beat him so severely that he would never offend again.'[12]

Shortly thereafter, one of the servants told Emily that she had once again found Keeper upstairs, 'lying on the best bed, in drowsy voluptuousness'.[13] At this unhappy news, Emily's face whitened with anger. She marched upstairs to deal with her errant dog and, moments later, as Charlotte and the servants observed:

> 'Down-stairs came Emily, dragging after her the unwilling Keeper, his hind legs set in a heavy attitude of resistance, held by the "scuft of his neck," but growling low and savagely all the time.'[14]

Emily took Keeper to a dark corner at the bottom of the stairs where, in a fit of temper, she administered a brutal beating. As Elizabeth Gaskell relates:

> 'Her bare clenched fist struck against his red fierce eyes, before he had time to make his spring, and, in the language of the turf, she "punished him" till his eyes were swelled up, and the half-blind, stupified beast was led to his accustomed lair, to have his swollen head fomented and cared for by the very Emily herself.'

The severity of this beating is certainly troubling – especially if it truly took place in the violent manner in which Gaskell and other nineteenth century reports have described it. Even so, the altercation seems to have had no effect on Keeper's devotion to Emily. He bore her no grudge and, as Gaskell states, 'loved her dearly ever after'.

Ever after was not a very long span of years for Emily Brontë. She died of consumption on 19 December 1848. Giving Keeper his evening meal was one of her very last acts the night before her death and, at her funeral, Keeper was first among the mourners who walked to her grave. In her 1883 biography of Emily, author Agnes Robinson describes the scene:

'They followed her to her grave – her old father, Charlotte, the dying Anne; and as they left the doors, they were joined by another mourner, Keeper, Emily's dog. He walked in front of all, first in the rank of mourners; and perhaps no other creature had known the dead woman quite so well. When they had lain her to sleep in the dark, airless vault under the church, and when they had crossed the bleak churchyard, and had entered the empty house again, Keeper went straight to the door of the room where his mistress used to sleep, and lay down across the threshold. There he howled piteously for many days; knowing not that no lamentations could wake her anymore.'

Keeper lived for three more years after Emily's death. Mr John Stores Smith, a visitor to Haworth in 1850, found him curled up asleep by the gate to the parsonage, old, toothless, and 'wholly blind'.[15] But even in his dotage, Keeper's indomitable spirit remained. Smith had brought his own dog with him to Haworth. Keeper's reaction to this young interloper is related by Smith in an 1868 edition of the *Free Lance*, a Manchester area newspaper:

'In the exuberance of his youth, with tail wagging and ears cocked, my dog trotted gaily up to this poor old memento of the past, and in a second there was such an uproar as Haworth churchyard had seldom or never heard. With an angry roar, the old dog, by sheer weight, rolled the younger one over, and commenced a painless worrying with his toothless gums; and the other, smarting under the first rebuff he had yet encountered, howled from vexation, rather than from pain. In a minute or less I had nipped up my animal and held him under my arm, barking furiously, while the old one rolled to and fro among the mandrakes, blindly seeking his vanished enemy.'

Keeper died the next year, in early December of 1851. By that time, Charlotte Brontë was the only Brontë sibling left. In a letter written on 8 December, she informed a friend of his passing, writing:

A painting of Emily Brontë's pet bulldog, Keeper, by Emily Brontë, 1838. (*Emily Brontë (British, 1818–1848), Keeper, 1838. Courtesy of the Brontë Society*)

The Brontë sisters, Anne. Emily, and Charlotte, painted by their brother, Patrick Branwell Brontë, 1834. (*Patrick Branwell Brontë (British, 1817–1848), The Brontë Sisters, Anne Brontë; Emily Brontë; Charlotte Brontë, 1834. Oil on canvas. © National Portrait Gallery, London*)

'Poor old Keeper (Emily's dog) died last Monday morning after being ill one night. He went gently to sleep; we laid his old faithful head in the garden. Flossy is dull, and misses him. There was something very sad in losing the old dog; yet I am glad he met a natural fate.'

The unique bond between Emily Brontë and Keeper inspired Elizabeth Gaskell to imagine that Keeper had gone on to a better place, perhaps reuniting with Emily at last in a manner not dissimilar from Cathy and Heathcliff at the end of *Wuthering Heights*. As Gaskell writes:

'Let us somehow hope, in half Red Indian creed, that he follows Emily now; and, when he rests, sleeps on some soft white bed of dreams, unpunished when he awakens to the life of the land of shadows.'

Chapter Seven

Looty the Pekingese and the
Destruction of the Summer Palace

'I have been able to retain a good many trifles that I bought there; also a pretty little dog, smaller than any King Charles, a real Chinese sleeve- dog. It has silver bells round its neck, and people say it is the most perfect little beauty they ever saw.'

Journal of Captain John Hart Dunne, 9 October 1860

With its flowing, silky coat, bowed legs and wide, flat muzzle, the diminutive Pekingese is one of the most easily recognizable dog breeds today. Pekingese were originally the exclusive pets of Chinese royalty. Penalties for taking one of them outside the bounds of the palace were severe, with some publications of the day claiming that apprehended Pekingese-nappers would face stoning or 'being cut into a thousand pieces'.[16] Such dire consequences were not enough to discourage British soldiers who, during the second Opium War, managed to carry away at least five of these little Lion Dogs of China and bring them safely back to Victorian Britain.

According to popular lore, British soldiers entered the seemingly empty Summer Palace at Peking in October of 1860. There they found five tiny Pekingese dogs huddled around the body of a lady – possibly the Emperor's aunt – who had committed suicide upon hearing the sound of the approaching troops. These little dogs were bundled up and taken back to England. Two of the dogs were commandeered by Admiral John Hay, eventually finding their way to Goodwood Castle where they would become the property of the Duke of Gordon. Two others were given to the Duchess of Richmond. The fifth dog, a fawn and white little beauty, was presented to Queen Victoria. The Queen christened the dog 'Looty'.

In actual fact, the events that led up to finding those little Pekingese were a bit different than the popular account and perhaps not as pleasant. On 6 October 1860, when French and British soldiers entered the Summer Palace at Peking, it was not a civilized enterprise culminating in the rescue of five helpless little dogs. It was a full-out sacking which ended with the Summer Palace being burned to the ground.

An account appearing in the 22 December 1860 edition of the *Illustrated Times* describes indiscriminate ransacking of public reception halls, state and private

Queen Victoria was known for her great love of dogs, a fact which inspired Captain John Hart Dunne to present her with Looty the Pekingese after the 1860 sacking of the Summer Palace in Peking. (*Anonymous Artist after Franz Xaver Winterhalter (German, 1805–1873), Queen Victoria, c. 1843. Oil on canvas. Courtesy National Gallery of Art, Washington*)

bedrooms, ante-rooms, boudoirs and every other apartment. Articles of value, including decorative lattice, jade ornaments, and rich clothing embroidered in gold thread, were either carried away by the invading army or destroyed. At the same time, orderly storerooms filled with expensive silks were torn asunder, the contents utilized to make tents and beds for the soldiers or used in place of rope to secure the priceless treasures that were carried away by the cartful.

Robert Swinhoe of Queen Victoria's Consular Service in China recounts the magnitude of the pillage and plunder in his *Narrative of the North China Campaign of 1860*, writing:,

'What a terrible scene of destruction presented itself! How disturbed now was the late quiescent state of the rooms, with their neat display of curiosities! Officers and men, English and French, were rushing about in a most unbecoming manner, each eager for the acquisition of valuables. Most of the Frenchmen were armed with large clubs, and what they could not carry away, they smashed to atoms.'

It was in all this that the five Pekingese dogs were found, though it is not clear whether they were 'running around in a distracted state,' as reported by the *Illustrated Times*, or in a private room cowering near the body of their dead mistress. A 1901 biographer of Queen Victoria offers a less distressing scenario, writing that:

'When the Summer Palace at Pekin was burning, this little dog [Looty] was discovered curled up amongst soft shawls and rugs in one of the wardrobes.'[17]

Looty and the other Pekingese were initially identified as 'Japanese Dogs', with many noting their resemblance to the King Charles spaniel. In fact, the variety of dog found at the Summer Palace was not officially called Pekingese until the beginning of the twentieth century. Up until then, it was known as either a Pekin or Chinese pug, Pekin or Chinese spaniel, or sometimes even a Chinese sleeve dog. Weighing only three pounds and touted as 'the smallest pet dog in the kingdom', Looty was a true sleeve dog as he could easily have been carried or concealed within the sleeves of one of the robes worn by a lady of the Chinese Imperial Household.[18] When Queen Victoria commissioned Friedrich Wilhelm Keyl to paint a portrait of Looty, it was noted that the little dog was so small that, in the end, the portrait of him was life-sized.

It is estimated that Looty was five years old when he was taken from the Summer Palace in Peking. He did not adjust well to his new life at Windsor

Castle. Relegated to the Windsor Kennels, he was too small and shy to fare well amongst the boisterous dogs in residence, with one publication even going so far as to suggest that the royal British canines took exception to his 'Oriental habits and appearance'.[19]

Despite his loneliness, Looty would live within the kennels at Windsor for another eleven years. It is unclear how much he interacted with Queen Victoria herself during that time, but upon his death in 1872, Looty received no ornate monument in the tradition of Eos and other favourite royal pets. The location of his grave is still unknown.

To show just how small Looty really was, Friedrich Wilhelm Keyl painted him next to other small objects, including an oriental vase, a bunch of flowers, and Looty's own belled collar which he had worn while living at the Summer Palace in Peking. (*Friedrich Wilhelm Keyl (German, 1823–1871), Looty, 1861. Oil on canvas. Royal Collection Trust ©Her Majesty Queen Elizabeth II, 2016/Bridgeman Images*)

The King Charles Spaniel was one of the most popular breeds of companion dog in the eighteenth and nineteenth centuries. (*Edouard Manet (French, 1832–1883), A King Charles Spaniel, c. 1866. Oil on linen. Courtesy National Gallery of Art, Washington*)

The head of a small, brown and white spaniel with a bell on its collar as portrayed by French Impressionist painter Auguste Renoir. (*Auguste Renoir (French, 1841–1919), Head of a Dog, 1870. Oil on canvas. Courtesy National Gallery of Art, Washington*)

Chapter Eight

The Bloodhounds Hired to Hunt Jack the Ripper

> '*Shall Jack the Ripper's art avail*
> *To battle Scotland-yard forsooth?*
> *Quick – on the flying murderer's trail*
> *Unleash the bloodhound, Truth!*'
>
> 'A Ballad of Bloodhounds',
> *Pall Mall Gazette,* 9 October 1888

In October of 1888, a series of brutal murders in Whitechapel prompted the London Metropolitan Police to consider hiring bloodhounds to hunt down the elusive killer we know today as Jack the Ripper. Four murders had already taken place in a fairly short span of time. Mary Ann Nichols was killed on 31 August, Annie Chapman was killed on 8 September, and in what has come to be known as the double event, the mutilated bodies of Elizabeth Stride and Catherine Eddowes were both found on 30 September. The public was panicked and the police were becoming desperate.

At the time, bloodhounds were not regularly used by the police. There were very few available who had the necessary training to assist them in tracking criminals. Nevertheless, bloodhounds had a great reputation for being able to scent out fugitives from justice. It was a reputation largely based on well-known – and sometimes exaggerated – incidents from the past, such as the 1876 tale of a bloodhound who sniffed out crucial evidence in the case of a murdered child. Members of the public reminded the police of these past cases, writing letters which they sent either directly to Scotland Yard or to the editors of popular newspapers like *The Times.* Newspapers often printed these letters, exerting further pressure on the police to hire a bloodhound or two to help solve the Ripper murders.

The Metropolitan Police responded to this pressure by contacting Mr Edwin Brough, a highly-respected breeder of bloodhounds in Wyndgate near Scarborough. After some negotiation, Mr Brough agreed to come to London. He brought with him two magnificent bloodhounds by the name of Barnaby and Burgho.

Barnaby was a four-year-old black and tan bloodhound by Nobleman out of Brevity. He was primarily a show dog at the time and, two years prior at the

The Bloodhound.

Though not regularly used by the police, bloodhounds of the Victorian era had a legendary reputation for hunting down criminals. (*after Sir Edwin Henry Landseer (British, 1802–1873), A Bloodhound with a Heavy Collar, nineteenth century. Steel engraving. Wellcome Library, London. Creative Commons Attribution 4.0 International Public License*)

Warwick Dog Show, had shared the 'Castle Park Stakes for man hunt with single hounds'.[20] Burgho was a two-year-old black and tan bloodhound by Maltravers out of Duchess of Ripple. Unlike Barnaby, Burgho had not been shown to a great extent, but he had been trained from a puppy to hunt 'the clean shoe' – meaning that he was capable of following the trail of a man whose shoes had not been treated in any way with applications of blood or other pungent preparations to aid in marking his trail.[21]

On 8 October 1888, at seven o'clock in the morning, Mr Brough brought Barnaby and Burgho to Regent's Park in London to perform the first of several trials for the Metropolitan Police. On that particular day, the ground was covered in frost. Even so, Barnaby and Burgho were able to successfully track, for nearly a mile, a young man who had been given fifteen minutes' lead.

Later that same evening, the two bloodhounds were taken to Hyde Park for another trial. The 10 October 1888 edition of the *Dundee Courier* describes the scene:

> 'It was, of course, dark, and the dogs were hunted in a leash, as would be the case if they were employed in Whitechapel. They were again successful in performing their allotted task and at seven o'clock yesterday morning a trial took place before Sir Charles Warren.'

Sir Charles Warren was, at the time, a rather controversial figure in London. Commissioner of the Metropolitan Police from 1886 until his resignation in 1888, Sir Charles was both criticized for his inability to capture Jack the Ripper and ridiculed for some of the methods he employed in trying to do so.

When, on the morning of 9 October 1888, Barnaby and Burgho performed their trial for Sir Charles, the press waited with bated breath, anxious to report on the slightest misstep. Instead, newspapermen of the day were obliged to acknowledge that all six of the runs made by Barnaby and Burgho were a success – even the two in which Sir Charles played the part of the hunted man himself. According to the 10 October 1888 edition of the *Yorkshire Post and Leeds Intelligencer*:

> 'In every instance the dogs hunted the persons, who were complete strangers to them, and occasionally the trail would be crossed. When this happened the hounds were temporarily checked, but either one or the other would pick up the trail again. In one of the longer courses the hounds were checked at half the distance; Burgho ran back, but Barnaby, moving a fresh cast forward, recovered the trail and ran the quarry home. The hound did this entirely unaided by his master, who thought that he was on the wrong track, but left him to his own devices. In consequence of the coldness

of the scent yesterday morning the hounds worked very slowly, but they demonstrated the possibility of tracking complete strangers on whose trail they had been laid.'

Sir Charles was quite pleased with the results of the trials. He decided that Barnaby and Burgho would be kept at the ready so that, if there were another murder, they could be summoned immediately and reach Whitechapel in 'less than half an hour'.[22]

The plan to use bloodhounds to track Jack the Ripper was not without its detractors. For example, a letter printed in the 8 October 1888 edition of the *St. James's Gazette* asserted that bloodhounds were merely 'fancy dogs', not suitable to be used as detectives, while an article in the 9 October 1888 edition of the same paper pointed out that bloodhounds would be useless unless the Ripper committed another murder.

An Illustration of Barnaby and Burgho, in an 1888 edition of the Penny Illustrated Paper. (*Sir Charles Warren's new criminal trackers: Mr Brough's bloodhounds being trained, nineteenth century. Engraving. Private Collection/© Look and Learn/Peter Jackson Collection/Bridgeman Images*)

SIR CHARLES WARREN'S NEW CRIMINAL TRACKERS: MR. BROUGH'S BLOODHOUNDS BEING TRAINED.

Even Jack the Ripper himself had a thing or two to say about the use of bloodhounds. In a letter delivered to Warren on 12 October, someone purporting to be the Ripper wrote, 'Dear Boss I hear you have bloodhounds for me now.'

Adding to all of these worries was the legitimate concern that Barnaby and Burgho would inadvertently cause an innocent man to be accused. The 9 October 1888 edition of the *St. James's Gazette* even declared that it was more likely that the two bloodhounds would 'bring an innocent butterman to bay' or run down a 'purveyor of cats'-meat' than it was they would catch the actual killer. It was not so much an error on the part of the dogs that was feared, but that some innocent person whom the dogs had misidentified would be overtaken by an angry mob of Whitechapel citizens and promptly torn to pieces. This was a very real possibility as the people living in Whitechapel were terrified and angry and, frustrated with the lack of progress by the police, more than ready to take the law into their own hands.

Unfortunately, Barnaby and Burgho would never get the chance to prove themselves. After the trials in the park, Mr Brough was compelled to return home to Wyndgate. Meanwhile, Burgho was sent to Brighton to compete in a dog show. Barnaby remained in London for a time in the care of Mr Brough's friend, Mr Taunton.

At the end of October, the Leman Street Police Station sent a telegram to Mr Taunton asking him to bring up Barnaby to help track a thief after a burglary. Mr Taunton complied. When he later wrote to inform Mr Brough of what he had done, Mr Brough was far from happy. He wired that Barnaby should be 'sent back at once' as there was a great danger that the dog might be poisoned if the criminal underworld learned that the police were using him to track burglars.[23]

Less than two weeks later, on 9 November 1888, Mary Jane Kelly was murdered in her lodgings at 13 Miller's Court. Sir Charles had previously ordered that if and when another murder took place, the crime scene was not to be disturbed until the bloodhounds had had a chance to pick up the scent. Inspector Abberline ordered the area to be cordoned off and policemen were posted outside of the room. They waited for two hours, at the end of which Abberline received word that the bloodhounds were no longer in London. Fearful that his prized dogs would be poisoned or otherwise killed by the Ripper, Mr Brough had taken Barnaby and Burgho home to Scarborough two weeks before.

Though theories on the identity of Jack the Ripper abound, the Whitechapel murders were never officially solved. Some people still believe that if Barnaby and Burgho had been available as originally planned, they might have been able to track down the mysterious man who accompanied Mary Kelly to her lodgings on that fateful morning in November. Mr Brough himself was doubtful. Interviewed many years later, he is quoted as saying that, despite his confidence in the skill of his bloodhounds, he 'had not much faith in the experiment'.[24]

Nevertheless, Mr Brough was quick to point out that his bloodhounds did appear to have had a deterrent effect. After all, Jack the Ripper committed no further crimes while Barnaby and Burgho remained in London. It was not until the two famous bloodhounds had been permanently removed to Scarborough that history's most notorious serial killer deigned to kill again.

A faithful dog stands at the door of his deceased owner's room. (*Emily Mary Osborne* (*British, 1828–1925*), *For the Last Time, 1864. Oil on canvas. Private Collection / Bridgeman Images*)

Chapter Nine

Dogs and Other Animals that Grieve

'The grave was closed in as usual, and next morning, "Bobby," as the dog is called, was found lying on the newly-made mound.'
London Evening Standard, 16 April 1867

During the nineteenth century, attributing human feelings to animals was generally considered to be more sentimentality than science. Nevertheless, Regency and Victorian era reports abound of dogs who wasted away at their master's graves, cats who refused to eat or drink upon the death of their mistress and even a pet monkey who committed suicide. Many of these stories were, indeed, mere sentimentalism. Others were poignant accounts of the behaviour of indisputably grief stricken animals.

Some of the most well-known stories of animal grief in the nineteenth century involve dogs. The most famous of these is the tale of Greyfriars' Bobby. Bobby was a small terrier (sometimes described as a 'Scotch' terrier and sometimes as a Skye terrier or Dandie Dinmont mix) whose owner died in the late 1850s and was subsequently buried in Greyfriars' churchyard in Edinburgh. Bobby is said to have been among the mourners at the funeral, but when the service was over, he did not leave the churchyard. Instead, he remained to keep watch over his master's grave. According to legend, he would continue keeping watch there for the next fourteen years, laying atop the grave each night 'regardless of the weather' until, one frozen winter morning, he was found dead, 'perished of age and cold'.[25]

There has since been some doubt cast on the tale of Bobby's unrelenting devotion to his master. In fact, a few newspapers of the day claim that Bobby never existed at all. Still others state that he was not a faithful dog mourning his deceased master, but merely a stray mongrel who wandered into Greyfriars' churchyard and, after being treated kindly by the Sexton, decided to make the churchyard his home.

But whether or not Bobby's story is factual has little bearing on the countless similar – albeit lesser known – tales involving other nineteenth century dogs that grieved for their deceased masters. These stories were reported in the nineteenth century news with some regularity. For example, a 10 February 1849 article in the *Norfolk News* relates the story of a spaniel whose mistress had taken deathly ill. The spaniel remained on his mistress' bed, 'occasionally emitting a melancholy howl,' until she passed away.

A particularly poignant Victorian era painting of a dog grieving the death of a small child. (*A. Archer, Dog Mourning Its Little Master, 1866.* © *City of Edinburgh Museums and Art Galleries, Scotland/Bridgeman Images*)

After his mistress's death, the spaniel's grief only increased. He kept vigil beside the coffin just as he had kept vigil beside his mistress's sickbed and 'would have been starved if his meals had not been taken to him'. On the day of the funeral, he followed along with the mourners to the churchyard. Afterward, he disappeared and was not seen again until well past midnight. It was then that he was discovered scratching at the door of his master's house, 'covered with soil' and 'greatly fatigued'. As the newspaper reports:

> 'It was found next day that he had visited the grave, and displaced a considerable quantity of the earth in his attempts to reach the coffin. He refuses food and is literally dying by inches.'

In another tale, not too dissimilar from that of Greyfriars' Bobby, a dog kept vigil at his master's grave for two long years. In this particular case, on the day of his master's burial, the dog took up residence in an 'aperture' near the grave that led to a gloomy little cavern wherein the dog would curl up, inconsolable, for days at a time.[26] A gentleman in a house across from the churchyard took pity on the poor creature and began to offer him food. The dog accepted the food, but he could not be lured from his owner's grave for long. As the 28 December 1858 edition of the *Northern Whig* relates:

'As soon as he had finished his hasty meal, he would gaze for a moment on his benefactor. It was an expressive look, but one which could not be misunderstood. It conveyed all the thanks that a broken heart could give. He then entombed himself once more for three or four days, when he crawled out again with his eyes sunk and his coat dishevelled. Two years he remained faithful to the memory of the being he had lost, and then having been missing several days, he was found dead in his retreat.'

Cats were not as popular as dogs in the nineteenth century, nor were they endowed with as many noble qualities. Even so, it was impossible for those in

A nineteenth century photograph of Greyfriars' Bobby. (*Greyfriars Bobby, nineteenth century. Photograph. Scottish National Portrait Gallery. Gift of Mrs. Riddell in memory of Peter Fletcher Riddell 1985*)

the nineteenth century not to recognize that cats were often capable of a great bond with their master or mistress and equally capable of grief at losing them. A 12 March 1887 edition of the *Leeds Times* reports the story of a cat who was found 'stretched dead' upon her mistress's grave, having apparently expired from 'excess of grief'.

Another report describes a little boy who was extraordinarily fond of his pet cat. When the boy grew ill, the cat 'attended him most devotedly'.[27] Later, when the boy died, the cat's grief was pitiful to behold. She disappeared from the family home, returning only once each evening at dinner time. It was subsequently discovered that she was spending all the rest of her time at the boy's grave, a poignant vigil which she would keep for the next five years until the boy's family moved away to another town, taking the grieving cat along with them.

Reports of animal grief in the nineteenth century were not limited to tales of pets grieving over the death of a human master or mistress. Many newspaper and magazine articles of the day reported stories of animals grieving deeply over the loss of an animal companion. As an example of this, a 29 May 1845 edition of the *Devizes and Wiltshire Gazette* published the story of two horses who had served together during the Peninsular War. These horses had drawn the same gun and had been 'inseparable companions through many battles'.

When one of the horses was killed on the battlefield, the survivor was brought back to the stable and put away as usual. However, when his food was brought to him, he refused to eat. Instead, he continually looked about for his lost companion, 'sometimes neighing as if to call him'. In the end, neither the presence of the other horses, nor the loving care of the soldiers, could console him. He died not many days later, having refused to eat a single bite after the death of his friend.

Some in the nineteenth century believed that, on occasion, an animal's grief went beyond the passive refusal of food or shelter and advanced to the animal actively hastening his own demise. Animal suicide, in fact. On 4 May 1889, the *Star* published an account of a gentleman in Paris who owned a very well trained pet monkey. During a bout of low spirits, the gentleman took his own life by shooting himself through the head. The unfortunate monkey was present during his master's suicide, observing every detail.

Later, when the doctor arrived to ascertain that the man was well and truly deceased, he found the lifeless body of the poor monkey stretched out next to his dead master 'with the revolver clasped between its fingers'. Imitating the actions of his master, the monkey had taken up the revolver and blown his brains out.

Today, the incident sounds more like mere mimicry than an instance of what the *Star* calls 'a double suicide' or 'suicide by grief'. Nevertheless, the story helps to illustrate the nineteenth century tendency to explain animal behaviour in terms of human emotion. Does this mean that all reports of animal grief in

Sir Edwin Henry Landseer depicts a a faithful dog remaining beside his master's coffin long after the other mourners have gone. (Sir Edwin Henry Landseer (*British, 1802–1873*), *The Old Shepherd's Chief Mourner, 1837. Oil on panel. Victoria & Albert Museum/Bridgeman Images*)

the nineteenth century were nothing more than anthropomorphism? Not at all. Modern animal behaviour experts have since proven what many in the nineteenth century sensed all along. Animals of every variety have the capacity to feel, to love and to grieve just as deeply in their own way as do human beings.

Fashionable ladies occasionally posed for portraits while holding a favorite cat. (*Jean-Baptiste Perroneau (French, 1715–1783), Magdaleine Pinceloup de la Grange, née de Parseval, 1747. Oil on canvas. Digital image courtesy of the Getty's Open Content Program*)

Part 11

Cats

Chapter Ten

Samuel Johnson's Favourite Cat

'A very fine cat, a very fine cat indeed.'
The Life of Samuel Johnson, James Boswell, 1791

D r Samuel Johnson, famed eighteenth century poet, essayist, moralist, and lexicographer, was a man known for his gentleness and humanity. He loved little children, often calling them his 'little dears' and showering them with sweetmeats, and he showed an uncommon sympathy and genuine concern for his servants.[28] But his kindness and consideration were not limited to human beings. He also had a great affection for animals, showing particular fondness for those that were under his care. His favourite of these was his cat, Hodge.

The majority of what has been written about Hodge over the last two hundred years is based on a few brief passages in James Boswell's 1791 biography *The Life of Samuel Johnson*. Boswell was Johnson's contemporary and had a chance to meet

Hodge himself. He was not overly fond of cats, admitting to having 'an antipathy' for them and to feeling 'uneasy' whenever one entered the room. As a result, he claimed to have 'suffered a good deal' as a result of seeing Hodge 'scrambling up Dr Johnson's breast, apparently with much satisfaction' while Johnson smiled and 'half-whistling, rubbed down his back, and pulled him by the tail'.

Samuel Johnson is best known for his *Dictionary of the English Language*, published in 1755. (*William Doughty (British, d. 1782) after Sir Joshua Reynolds (British, 1723–1792), Samuel Johnson, 1779. Mezzotint. Courtesy National Gallery of Art, Washington*)

A portrait of Scottish biographer James Boswell, who wrote about Hodge in his 1791 biography of Samuel Johnson. (*Print made by John Jones (British, ca. 1745–1797), James Boswell of Auchinleck, Esq., 1786. Mezzotint on very thin, smooth, cream laid paper. Yale Center for British Art, Paul Mellon Fund*)

Boswell's aversion to the feline race did not prevent him from observing that Hodge was 'a fine cat,' a statement to which Johnson famously replied:

> "'Why, yes, Sir, but I have had cats whom I liked better than this" and then as if perceiving Hodge to be out of countenance, adding, "but he is a very fine cat, a very fine cat indeed."'

According to Boswell, Johnson was quite happy to indulge Hodge. He allowed him the run of his rooms off of Fleet Street and tempted him with the tastiest foods. Oysters were a particular favourite of Hodge and Johnson himself would go to the market to procure them. He worried that if he ordered the servants to do so, they would come to resent Hodge for making extra work for them.

Johnson's affection for cats was not limited to Hodge. He had other pet cats over the years, including a 'white kitling' by the name of Lily.[29] He was fond of them all and quite protective. On one occasion, he is reported to have reprimanded his wife for beating a pet cat in front of a housemaid 'lest she should give a precedent for cruelty'.[30] On another occasion, Johnson remarked with some disfavour upon the 'despicable state of a young gentleman of good family' who had taken to 'running about town shooting cats'.[31] After relating this incident, Boswell writes that Johnson fell into 'a sort of kindly reverie,' wherein he thought of his own favourite cat – a recollection which prompted him to declare, 'But Hodge shan't be shot: no, no, Hodge shall not be shot.'

There is no other mention of Hodge in Boswell's biography. However, the poet Percival Stockdale writes about Hodge in his 1809 memoirs, remarking on the tremendous affection that Johnson had for his cat:

> 'I have frequently seen the ruggedness of Dr Johnson softened to smiles, and caresses; by the inarticulate, yet pathetic expressions of his favourite Hodge…'

The actual date of Hodge's death is in some dispute. Depending on the source, he is reported to have passed away anytime between 1764 and 1773. What we do know is that Johnson remained with his cat during his final hours. He even procured valerian – a medicinal plant with sedative properties – and administered it to Hodge in order to ease his pain.

Upon Hodge's death, Stockdale published an epitaph in his honour titled 'An Elegy on the Death of Dr Johnson's Favourite Cat'. It is in this elegy that we are first given a hint as to what Hodge might have looked like. As Stockdale writes:

> 'Who, by his master when caressed
> Warmly his gratitude expressed;
> And never failed his thanks to purr,
> Whene'er he stroked his sable furr?'

In 1997, Hodge was commemorated with a bronze statue in Gough Square, London. Created by sculptor Jon Bickley, it shows Hodge sitting atop Samuel Johnson's dictionary with empty oyster shells at his feet. The placard on the base of the statue reads in part: 'Hodge a very fine cat indeed belonging to Samuel Johnson (1709–1784) of Gough Square.'

The first cat show at the Crystal Palace boasted a variety of exotic felines, including Persians, Siamese, and a Wild Cat, somewhat similar to the one shown in this 1850 painting by famed French animal artist Rosa Bonheur. (*Rosa Bonheur* (*French, 1822–1899*), *Wild Cat, 1850. Oil on canvas. Nationalmuseum, Stockholm*)

A black and white kitten swats at dominoes in this nineteenth century painting by animal artist Henriette Ronner-Knip. (*Henriette Ronner* (*Dutch, 1821–1909*), *Kitten's Game, ca. 1860–1878. Oil on panel. Rijksmuseum, Amsterdam. Bequest of Mr. Wester JBAM Woudt, Haarlem*)

Chapter Eleven

The Cat Show at the Crystal Palace

'The Cat Show ought to be under the patronage of spinsters & the judges should be selected from maiden ladies.'

Birmingham Daily Mail, 15 May 1871

In 1871, at the instigation of cat fancier Harrison Weir, the first ever cat show was held in England. The concept was a novel one. At the time, there were no breed registries for cats and no precise standards on which to judge them. However, Weir was nothing if not persuasive. Within days of having first broached the subject with the manager of the Crystal Palace in Sydenham, London, Weir presented his full scheme, including the schedule of prizes, price of entry, number of classes, and even the points by which the cats would be judged.

The cats were to be divided into different varieties of colour, form, size and sex. Coat patterns such as tabby and tortoiseshell would also be represented. All

The Crystal Palace was originally erected in Hyde Park to house the Great Exhibition of 1851. (*E. J. Stanley, The Crystal Palace in Hyde Park, 1852. Watercolour, white gouache, black chalk and graphite on medium, slightly textured, cream wove paper. Yale Center for British Art, Paul Mellon Collection*)

that remained was to find the cats to participate in the show. With no breeders to approach and a lack of people willing to part with their pet cats for any length of time, Weir and the representatives of the Crystal Palace 'went forth into the highways and byways on the lookout for presentable animals'.[32]

A drawing of a black, cat's head which illustrated the posting bill for the 1871 cat show at the Crystal Palace. (*Cat Head Drawing Advertisement for the Crystal Palace Cat Show, 1871. Our Cats and All About Them by Harrison William Weir, 1889*)

Despite their efforts, the quota of cats necessary for the cat show had still not been met. An article in the 1891 issue of *Pearson's Magazine* relates how this shortage was resolved. It reads in part:

'Then someone discovered that the Palace cellars were full of cats and kittens and mice, so a few workmen were set to work cat-hunting there. The workmen also brought their own cats to the show.'

The domestic cats on display were supplemented by examples of cats both rare and exotic. There was a Manx from the Isle of Man, a Persian cat 'direct from Persia', and an enormous English cat weighing in at twenty-one pounds who was reported to be 'the biggest in the show'.[33] Of particular note, the first two Siamese cats ever seen in the country were also on exhibit. An 1871 edition of *Harper's Weekly* describes them as:

'Soft, fawn-coloured creatures, with jet-black legs – an unnatural, nightmare kind of cat, singular and elegant in their smooth skins, and ears tipped with black, and blue eyes with red pupils.'

Perhaps the most exciting addition to the cat show was a British wildcat exhibited by the Duke of Sutherland. According to *Harper's Weekly*, this variety of wildcat was almost extinct in the British Isles. And the duke's cat was truly wild, leading *Harper's Weekly* to declare that:

'He behaved like a mad devil, and ten men could not get him into a wire cage
out of the box in which he was sent.'

The 1871 issue of *Lippincott's Monthly Magazine* reports that there were 211 cats
on exhibition at the cat show at the Crystal Palace, many of them 'torn from their
domestic hearths'. *Harper's Weekly* reports a lower number, stating that there were
160 specimens of cat at the cat show. Regardless of the precise number, the event
required that those 150-plus cats remain in their cages and on public display.

The wire-front cages were arranged in two rows, back to back. The public
was then ushered into the event in a long line and made to walk slowly up one
row and down the other, all under the watchful eye of a policeman. According to
Lippincott's Monthly Magazine:

Visitors to the first cat show at the Crystal Palace admire some of the winning cats in this
illustration from an 1871 edition of the Penny Illustrated Paper. (*Cat Show at the Crystal
Palace, Penny Illustrated Paper, 22 July 1871. ©The British Library Board. All rights reserved.
With thanks to The British Newspaper Archive*)

'If any lingered by some more attractive cat, the man in authority cried out, as in the streets of London, "Move on!"'

Harrison Weir believed the cats to be perfectly content in their temporary confinement. Describing the scene that met his eyes upon arriving at the Crystal Palace the morning of the cat show, he states:

'Instead of the noise and struggles to escape, there lay the cats in their different pens, reclining on crimson cushions, making no sound save now and then a homely purring, as from time to time they lapped the nice new milk provided for them.'[34]

Other reports did not paint such a pretty picture. It was the month of July and the summer heat had made the cats depressed and dull. Many of them were sleeping with their backs turned to the public. Those people who had come all the way to view the cats were not amused. Determined to rouse the unresponsive felines, they poked them with their fingers, canes and even their parasol points. As one publication reports:

'They kept stirring them up with their fingers and parasol-points till some people cried "Shame!" On the whole, though, we agreed that the cats liked it; it prevented them feeling so dull.'[35]

In addition to complaints about the cats being dull, there were many complaints about the ordinary appearance of some of the cats. The following paragraph is a particularly vitriolic report from Prentice Mulford of *Lippincott's Monthly Magazine*. Reading between the lines, one can't help but think that his ire is directed as much at the working-class humans who attended the cat show as at their similarly plebeian cats. He writes:

'Some were very shabby-looking cats, apparently more familiar with the cellars than the parlours of London. They belonged to the lower feline orders. They seemed of that class often to be seen in cities sleeping by day in the charred apartments of partly-burned buildings, fur rough and slovenly, eyes sore and watery, holding themselves in low estimate, lacking dignity and self-respect...'

The poor and working-class owners of these shabby-looking cats had no doubt been persuaded to enter their pets in the cat show in hopes of winning some of the more than £70 in prizes offered by the directors of the Crystal Palace. The prizes were chiefly in money. However, some ladies had offered special prizes

Manx, or Tailless Cat
British Wild Cat

Persian Cat
English Cat—the Biggest in the Show

Siamese Cats
French-African Cat

PRIZE CATS

An 1871 illustration in the Graphic shows some of the cats that competed at the first cat show, including a Manx, a Persian, two Siamese, a French-African cat, a British Wildcat, and an English cat described as the biggest at the show. (*Prize Cats, The Graphic, 22 July 1871.* © *The British Library Board. All rights reserved. With thanks to The British Newspaper Archive*)

'to encourage the poor to be kind' to their cats and to 'feed them well'.[36] These prizes included such random odds and ends as a teakettle, a teapot, a mug, and a framed photograph of a cat.

At the close of the cat show, *Harper's Weekly* pronounced the event 'a complete success'. They predicted that it would soon be imitated, spawning cat shows throughout the country. They were not wrong. The cat show at the Crystal Palace would become an annual event with attendance and participation growing with each subsequent year. Cat shows in other venues followed. The shows did much to improve the public perception of cats. Unfortunately, though many of the public saw much to admire in a fancy Persian or a sleek Siamese, the prejudice against the domestic cat was still quite strong.

Nevertheless, the very novelty of the first cat show caught the public's imagination. It caught the imagination of writers as well and many incorporated anecdotes about the cat show into their stories. The 1877 book *Only a Cat* by Mrs. Henry H.B. Paull is narrated by the cat himself. In it, he relates the effect the cat show has had on his species and on the estimation in which cats were held by society in general:

> 'Instead of being treated with contempt, dislike, or even cruelty, as in days now happily gone by, there is a talk of our being exhibited in shows at the Crystal Palace, and those of us who are well fed and kindly treated, are standing proofs that we are not the spiteful, treacherous creatures our enemies so falsely represent.'

In 1887, Harrison Weir founded The National Cat Club. It was the first cat registry of its kind in the world. In the following years, many more cat registries would spring up, including the Cat Fancier's Association (CFA) in the United States. Today, cat shows are filled with pedigreed cats of every description from Persians and Siamese to British Shorthairs and Maine Coons. It is a very different scene from that at the Crystal Palace nearly 130 years ago. And yet, without that first cat show, with its motley collection of workmen's cats and cats found in the basement, who knows what the world of purebred cats would look like today?

The cat show at the Crystal Palace proved so popular that it was repeated the next year. (*Show for Cats at the Crystal Palace, Penny Illustrated Paper, 18 May 1872.* © *The British Library Board. All rights reserved. With thanks to The British Newspaper Archive*)

A woman is shown holding her tabby cat in this 1875 portrait. (*Auguste Renoir (French, 1841–1919, Woman with a Cat, c. 1875. Oil on canvas. National Gallery of Art, Washington*)

Eighteenth and nineteenth century paintings of cats often depicted them getting into some sort of mischief. (*Henriette Ronner (Dutch, 1821–1909), The Musicians, ca. 1876–1877. Watercolour over a light pencil sketch. Rijksmuseum, Amsterdam. Bequest of Esq. PA van den Velden, The Hague*)

Chapter Twelve

The Case of the Victorian Cat Ladies

'Old maids and cats have long been proverbially associated together, and rightly or wrongly these creatures have been looked upon with a certain degree of suspicion and aversion by a large proportion of the human race.'

Dundee Courier, 5 October 1880

For centuries, maiden ladies and cats have been inextricably linked in the public mind. This was especially true in the eighteenth and nineteenth centuries. Newspaper reports and magazine articles of the day ridiculed spinsters for indulging their cats, criticizing them for everything from the purchase of expensive cat foods to more eccentric extravagances, such as holding elaborate cat weddings and cat funerals. Of these, perhaps the most common complaint levied against elderly spinsters was that they tended to accumulate cats by the dozen – often to the detriment of their friends, families, and neighbours.

In August of 1886, an elderly maiden lady by the name of Miss Ann Lloyd was summoned to Solihull Police Court at the insistence of Mr William Harris, Inspector of Nuisances for the Solihull Rural Sanitary Authority. Miss Lloyd lived at Llandudno House, Sparkhill, along with her two spinster sisters and a large group of cats, the number of which was later disputed in court. Harris alleged that these cats had created a nuisance in the form of a deeply offensive smell which emanated outward from the Lloyd sisters' house and into the houses of their neighbours. Miss Lloyd, in turn, defended herself by repeatedly insisting that she and her sisters had no cats at all.

The issue first arose in September of that year when Harris began to receive complaints from the Lloyd sisters' neighbours about an offensive smell at Llandudno House. In response to these complaints, he visited the sisters on 20 August 1886 where, according to an article in the 29 September 1886 edition of the *Aberdeen Press and Journal*:

'On entering the house there was a terrible stench, evidently from the cats. [Harris] was invited into the front room, and he remained there for some time, but eventually he was compelled to leave the apartment and go into the backyard on account of the fearful stench.'

A MAIDEN LADY AND HER FAMILY.

Pub⁴ by O.Hodgson 10.Cloth Fair, London

Maiden ladies and their often outrageous collections of pets were the subject of many humorous illustrations in both the eighteenth and nineteenth centuries. (Print made by unknown artist, (G. T. W.), Published by Orlando Hodgson (*British, active 1820–1840*), *A Maiden Lady and her Family, between 1820 and 1840. Lithograph with watercolour on moderately thick, slightly textured, beige wove paper. Yale Center for British Art, Paul Mellon Collection*)

The 27 September 1886 edition of the *Daily Gazette for Middlesbrough* reports that the stench in the drawing room was so great that Harris 'became sick'. While an article in the same day's issue of the *Birmingham Daily Post* quotes Harris as testifying:

> 'I must really say that I have had to go amongst many bad smells, but none so bad as this. While I remained in the front room the perspiration poured off me.'

Harris would later go on to explain that not only was the house filthy, but that, at the time of his visit, the sisters were boiling 'fish offal' on the stove to feed to their cats. They were also boiling cabbage for their own dinner. The cats themselves were not present in the house at the time of his visit. However, upon withdrawing to the Lloyd sisters' small back garden, the *Aberdeen Press and Journal* reports that Harris saw 'a large number of cats'. Similarly the *Daily Gazette* states that, in the Lloyds' garden '…the stench was almost as bad, and in the yard [Harris] found six or seven cats.'

The precise number of cats owned by the Lloyd sisters would become a primary issue when the case came before the police court. None of the witnesses seemed entirely sure exactly how many cats were in residence as the wily felines were continually on the move. The *Birmingham Daily Post* quotes an exchange between Mr Chattock, the magistrate, and Mr Harris which reads in part:

> 'Mr Chattock: How many?

> 'Witness: I couldn't count them. They were going about in all directions.

> 'Mr Chattock: Did you try to count them?

> 'Witness: I saw six or seven run by me into the back kitchen, where there were two pots of fish offal boiling for them.'

Harris further testified that the stench in Llandudno House was 'plainly perceptible in the next house'. Part of this was due to the potency of the stench and part was due to the unfortunate architecture of the houses in that neighbourhood. They were 'jerry-built' of cheap and insubstantial materials and the smell 'easily penetrated the walls'.

Harris served the Lloyd sisters with a notice on 22 August and told them to get rid of their cats. At first, Miss Lloyd claimed that she and her sisters had no cats (an assertion repeated throughout the case). She then stated that they had only

EXTRAORDINARY COLLECTION OF CATS.—A LADY AND HER MENAGERIE.

The *Illustrated Police News* depicts a cat hoarding case from 1867. (*Extraordinary Collection of Cats, Illustrated Police News, June 1, 1867.* ©*The British Library Board. All rights reserved. With thanks to The British Newspaper Archive*)

six cats, but that those cats were restricted to the back garden and never stepped foot in the house. When Harris questioned Miss Lloyd about the rest of the cats seen racing about the premises, the *Daily Gazette* reports that Miss Lloyd claimed that they 'only kept six cats, and that all the others which [Harris] saw about were merely "visitors."'

In the following weeks, letters from angry neighbours continued to pour in and, on 15 September, Harris was obliged to pay yet another call at Llandudno House. There, he found that the stench was unabated. It was then that the sisters were summoned to the police court to answer to the magistrate.

At the police court, Harris testified at length about the state of the Lloyd sisters' house and the sickening quality of the stench. He also gave his opinion that the Lloyd sisters were running a sort of cat hospital for cats that had been abused by neighbourhood boys. How the court felt about this theory is unclear since most of the reporting seems to focus on the horrendously bad smell. To that end, a neighbour of the Lloyd sisters, a man by the name of Mr Austin, also testified, stating:

> 'The smell was bad both day and night, and he could hardly live in the house. He saw one of the sisters, and complained to her of the nuisance, but it had no effect. Witness was obliged at night to sleep with all the doors and windows open in consequence of the fearful stench which pervaded the premises. When he spoke to Miss Lloyd about the matter she assured him that they had no cats.'[37]

Miss Lloyd was indignant and regularly interrupted the testimony to rebuke the witnesses. In one instance, the *Birmingham Daily Post* reports that she addressed Austin demanding:

> 'How can you speak so falsely of us, when you put my sister out of the house, and hurt us very much indeed? And we have never had a cat in the house, I'll take my oath.'

In another exchange, while Austin was testifying, Miss Lloyd declared:

> 'It is impossible for a cat that has its liberty and has never been in our house, to smell through your wall.'

When given a chance to call a witness of her own, Miss Lloyd called Police Constable White – the officer who had served the summons – expecting that he would state that the smell was not as bad as it had so far been made out. Unfortunately, White's testimony would be some of the most mortifying of all for poor Miss Lloyd. The *Birmingham Daily Post* reports the following exchange between Mr Chattock and Constable White:

> 'Mr Chattock (to the witness): You can say there was an offensive smell?

> 'Witness: There was, your worships, but I don't know what it came from. I have thought perhaps it was from the ladies' bodies.'

This exchange was followed by loud laughter from the gallery – laughter in which the magistrate joined. Such a reaction did not bode well for Miss Lloyd's case. When he was done laughing at her expense, the magistrate proposed to adjourn the case until 9 October in order to give Miss Lloyd and her sisters another chance to abate the nuisance. However, when Miss Lloyd, continued to claim that there was no nuisance, the magistrate 'made a peremptory order for its abatement within ten days'.

Ultimately, the Lloyd sisters did not comply with the magistrate's order, at least, not within the time given. A 6 December 1886 edition of the *Birmingham Daily Post* reports another case involving Miss Lloyd and her neighbour Mr Austin at the Solihull Police Court. Austin was summoned before the court by an inspector for the Birmingham Society for the Prevention of Cruelty to Animals to answer to the charge of 'unlawfully beating and ill-treating a cat, belonging to Ann Lloyd of Llandudno Villa, Sparkhill, on November 14.'

In this case, Miss Lloyd no longer denied that she had cats in her home. In fact, she admitted to taking in abused strays and nursing them back to health, after which she claimed to find homes for them. As for Mr Austin and his cat abuse, though the court acknowledged that he did strike Miss Lloyd's cat, he suffered no penalty for his crime other than court costs. And, once again, the testimony about the Lloyd sisters and their cats engendered a great deal of laughter from the court.

Though the case of the cat hoarding spinsters at Llandudno House generated 'an unusual degree of interest' in the Victorian era, it was not entirely unique among court actions featuring old maids and their cats.[38] Neighbours frequently complained about feline nuisances and, when these actions came to court, the public looked on with a great deal of amusement. The more eccentric the spinster – or, as in some cases, the elderly bachelor – the greater the degree of laughter.

As the century came to a close, however, both the courts and the Victorian public began to look on animal related issues with a little less humour. Laws were passed, animal welfare groups were formed, and various rescue homes were founded, including the Home for Starving and Forsaken Cats at Gordon Cottage, Hammersmith in 1895 and the Royal Institution for Starving Cats in Camden Town in 1896. Even so, the popular stereotype of old maids and their cats persisted, lasting well into the twentieth century and beyond.

A black and white cat is portrayed hunting in a meadow in this 1887 painting. (*Bruno Liljefors (Swedish, 1860–1939), Cat on a Flowery Meadow, 1887. Oil on canvas. Nationalmuseum, Stockholm*)

Four cats patiently wait for a dish of hot milk to cool. (*Elisabeth Fearn Bonsall (American, 1861–1956), Hot Milk, 1896. Oil on canvas. Courtesy of the Pennsyvania Academy of the Fine Arts, Philadelphia. Joseph E. Temple Fund*)

Chapter Thirteen

Cat Funerals in the Victorian Era

'For three days pussy, whose remains were placed with loving care in a beautiful brass-bound oaken coffin, with inner linings of silk and wool, lay in state in the drawing-room.'

Hull Daily Mail, 1 April 1897

The Victorian fascination with death is well evidenced in the elaborate mourning rituals of the era, including extravagant funerals, black-edged mourning stationery and mourning fashions and jewellery. But not all of these mourning rituals were performed in honour of deceased humans. Some were performed in honour of deceased pets. Victorian era animal lovers of every social class, from the poorest village spinster to Queen Victoria herself, held ceremonies for favourite pets who had passed away or erected memorial headstones and monuments for dear departed animal friends.

Of all the animals buried and mourned in the Victorian era, it was dogs who received the lion's share of the funerary honours. Cats, however, were not left completely out in the cold. Bereaved cat owners commissioned undertakers to build cat caskets. Clergymen performed cat burial services. And stone masons chiselled cat names on cat headstones. Many in society viewed these types of ceremonies as no more than an amusing eccentricity of the wealthy or as yet another odd quirk of the elderly spinster. Others were deeply offended that an animal of any kind should receive a Christian burial.

On 10 March 1894, the *Cheltenham Chronicle* reported the story of a Kensington lady 'of distinction' who held a funeral for her cat, Paul. This function was conducted just as if it had been 'the interment of a human person of some importance'. As the newspaper relates:

'A respectable undertaker was called in, and instructed to conduct the funeral in the ordinary way; the body was to be enclosed in a shell which would go inside a fine oak coffin. There were the usual trappings, including a plate on which was inscribed the statement that "Paul" had for seventeen years been the beloved and faithful cat of Miss – , who now mourned his loss in suitable terms. The coffin, with a lovely wreath on it, was displayed in the undertaker's shop, where it was an object of intense interest and not a little amusement.'

Though Paul's burial service was not sanctioned by the Church, this did not stop other cat funerals from adopting a religious tone. The 1 April 1897 edition of the *Hull Daily Mail* relates the story of a clergyman who held a funeral for his cat. This particular cat is described as an obese, black and white female who was known to go for daily walks with her master. Upon her death, the clergyman and his household were 'thrown into mourning'. The *Hull Daily Mail* states:

'For three days pussy, whose remains were placed with loving care in a beautiful brass-bound oaken coffin, with inner linings of silk and wool, lay in state in the drawing-room. At the termination of this period, the rev. gentleman hired a cab, drove to the station, and took a train for the North, bearing with him the oak coffin and the precious remains. Where the funeral took place seems to be somewhat of a mystery – at least there are conflicting accounts – but of one thing people seem to be certain. The ceremonial respect which had been accorded to the deceased was maintained to the last, and the burial service, or part thereof, was recited at pussy's grave.'

Maiden ladies and their cats were a frequent subject of caricature, such as in this 1789 print which shows a line of old maids attending a cat's funeral. (*John Pettit after Frederick George Byron (British, 1764–1792), Old Maids at a Cats Funeral, 10 April 1789. Etching and stipple with watercolour. Wellcome Library, London. Creative Commons Attribution 4.0 International Public License*)

Most historical reports on cat funerals from the Victorian era are recounted with humour. Others show a darker response to pet burials. An article in the 17 September 1885 issue of the *Edinburgh Evening News* relates the story of a very old woman in Abercromby Street intent on giving her deceased cat, Tom, a decent burial. She applied to the local undertaker to build Tom a suitable coffin and employed a gravedigger, by the name of Jamie, to dig a grave for Tom in the local burying ground. As the article states:

> 'The funeral, which took place in the afternoon yesterday, was largely attended. Miss – carried the coffin, and on the way to the graveyard the crowd of youngsters who followed became exceedingly noisy, and being apprehensive that the affair would end in a row, "Jamie" closed the iron gate with the view of preventing any but a select few from entering. The crowd, however, became even more excited, scaled the wall, hooting and yelling vociferously, crying that it was a shame and a disgrace to bury a cat like a Christian.'

Whether this uproar was truly a result of outrage over Tom being buried like a Christian or simply an excuse for rowdy youths to misbehave is unclear. Regardless, the results of the riot that ensued were exceedingly unpleasant for Tom's elderly, bereaved owner. The *Edinburgh Evening News* reports:

> 'The coffin was afterwards smashed, and the body of the cat taken out, and ultimately the uproar became so great that the police had to be called to protect the gravedigger and the old lady. The latter managed to get hold of the dead body of Tom, and with the assistance of Constables Johnston and Smith escaped into a house in the neighbourhood, where she remained for some time. In Abercromby Street, where she resides, a number of policemen had to be kept on duty till a late hour in order to protect her from the violence of the crowd.'

Perhaps the main cause of outrage lies in the fact that Tom's owner was attempting to bury a cat in the human graveyard. This was not an uncommon complaint. Many graveyards did not allow pets to be buried in consecrated ground. As a result, pet cemeteries were established. One of the most well-known was the Hyde Park Dog Cemetery, opened in 1881. As the name denotes, this was primarily a burial ground for dogs. However, it also admitted the corpses of three pet monkeys and two cats.

Other pet cemeteries existed throughout Victorian England, both public and private. The pet cemetery at the Essex seat of Sir Thomas Lennard had pet monuments dating as far back as the 1850s, while the pet cemetery at Edinburgh Castle originated as a burial place for nineteenth century regimental mascots and officers' dogs. Even the author Thomas Hardy had a pet cemetery at his home at Max Gate in Dorchester in which all but one of the headstones were carved with the famous novelist's own hands.

The majority of headstones and monuments in pet cemeteries of that era are for dogs. Dogs were incredibly popular pets during the nineteenth century. They were typically viewed as selfless, devoted friends and guardians, while cats were, to some extent, still seen as sly, self-serving opportunists. Add to that Queen Victoria's own preference for the canine race and it is easy to see why dogs came to be the preferred animal companion of the era.

This bias in favour of dogs had no effect on Victorian cat fanciers whatsoever. Cat funerals continued to take place with just as much pomp and ceremony as dog funerals. The public reaction to both was very much the same; amusement, outrage and occasionally scorn. One example of the latter is from an article in the 17 August 1880 edition of the *Portsmouth Evening News* which reports on a lady who sent out 'black-edged funeral cards' upon the death of her dog. As a sort of disclaimer, the article states, 'It is superfluous to affirm that the owner of that lamented Fido is a maiden lady.'

It does seem that a great many reports of pet funerals in the nineteenth century news involve some stereotypical variety of spinster. Though humorous, this was not always the norm. The simple fact is that, throughout history, there have been people who have grieved at the loss of their pets. During the Victorian era, this grief took shape in elaborate pet funerals. For cats, who were still persecuted in so many ways, these ceremonies seem especially poignant.

George Stubbs' famous 1762 portrait of the Marquis of Rockingham's racehorse, Whistlejacket. (*George Stubbs* (*British, 1724–1806*), *Whistlejacket, 1762. Oil on canvas. National Gallery, London, UK/Bridgeman Images*)

Part III

Horses and Farm Animals

Chapter Fourteen

Whistlejacket and Eighteenth Century Equine Artist George Stubbs

'Whistlejacket had a temper so savage that only one man could be trusted to take him to and from his stable.'
Memoirs of Thomas Dodd, William Upcott, and George Stubbs, R.A., 1879

George Stubbs was the preeminent horse painter of eighteenth century England. Not only was he an incredibly skilled artist, he had a wealth of scientific knowledge as well. He lectured on anatomy at York Hospital and he authored the internationally acclaimed book *Anatomy of the Horse.* Unsurprisingly, he was a painter greatly sought after by those in possession of the finest bloodstock. One such person was Charles Watson-Wentworth, the 2nd Marquis of Rockingham, who, in 1762, commissioned Stubbs to paint a life-size portrait of his Thoroughbred racehorse, Whistlejacket.

Whistlejacket was an uncommonly beautiful chestnut stallion with a flaxen mane and tail. He looked little like the Thoroughbred horses of today. In fact, with his refined features and small, elegant head, he has often been mistakenly identified as an Arabian. This is not entirely inaccurate. Whistlejacket's grandsire was, in fact, the Godolphin Arabian, one of the three foundation sires of the Thoroughbred horse breed.

A self-portrait of eighteenth century equine artist George Stubbs from 1759. (*George Stubbs (British, 1724–1806), Self-Portrait, ca. 1759. Oil on copper. Yale Center for British Art, Paul Mellon Fund*)

Whistlejacket's beauty was eclipsed only by his notoriously evil temperament. He was a vicious and frequently unmanageable stallion, described as having 'a temper so savage that only one man could be trusted to take him to and from his stable'.[39] It was this man who would bring Whistlejacket out to Stubbs each day so that he could work on his portrait of the beautiful horse. These sessions were fairly uneventful – that is, until the very last day.

The final sitting for Whistlejacket's portrait proved to be shorter than Stubbs had anticipated. His work was finished well before the time fixed for Whistlejacket's trusted groom to come and lead him away. While the boy holding Whistlejacket waited, Stubbs took the opportunity to put his nearly completed painting into the light so that he could examine its effect. It was then that, for the first time, Whistlejacket caught sight of the life-size painting of himself. An 1879 account describes the ensuing scene as follows:

'The boy, who was leading Whistlejacket up and down, called out suddenly, and, turning, Stubbs saw the horse staring at his own portrait and quivering with rage. He sprang forward to attack it, rearing, and lifting the boy off his legs. Very hard work they had to preserve the picture.'[40]

The painting of Whistlejacket was originally intended to be a royal portrait featuring King George III. Stubbs had been commissioned to paint only the horse and, when he had finished, a landscape painter was to be hired to paint the background and then a portrait painter to paint the king astride the great chestnut stallion. However, when the Marquis of Rockingham heard the story of Whistlejacket's reaction to the life-size painting of himself, he was so pleased that:

'He would not allow a single touch to be added, but framed and hung the painting without a background.'[41]

Whistlejacket was approximately thirteen years old at the time his portrait was painted in 1762. His racing career was over and he had been retired to stud. The details of the remainder of his life are unknown. It is not clear when he died or where he is buried. Nevertheless, he has not been forgotten. In addition to being depicted in the famous life-size painting, he was also portrayed in another Stubbs' painting in 1762 along with the Marquis of Rockingham's head groom, Mr Cobb and two other stallions of the stud at Wentworth Park. As if that were not enough to gain him immortality, Whistlejacket's name has been forever preserved within the pages of the classic 1773 Oliver Goldsmith play *She Stoops to Conquer* wherein the character of Tony Lumpkin declares, 'I have got you a pair of horses that will fly like Whistlejacket ...'

George Stubbs himself would live on to the ripe old age of eighty-one. Today, his horse paintings are considered some of the finest examples of equestrian art in existence. They feature in various private collections and museums around the world, including the National Gallery in London where the painting of Whistlejacket is currently on display.

Eighteenth and nineteenth century race horses and coach horses were generally painted in profile, as in this Stubbs' portrait of a young chestnut stallion named Pumpkin. (*George Stubbs (British, 1724–1806), Pumpkin with a Stable-lad, 1774. Oil on panel. Yale Center for British Art, Paul Mellon Collection*)

Horses were often portrayed standing with their groom or with a stable lad. (*George Stubbs (British, 1724–1806), Phaeton with a Pair of Cream Ponies and a Stable-Lad, between 1780 and 1784. Oil on panel. Yale Center for British Art, Paul Mellon Collection*)

Chapter Fifteen

An 1828 Balloon Ascent ... On a Pony!

'The balloon, to be sure, went up; but what is a balloon without a pony?'
Morning Chronicle, 16 August 1828

In 1828, famed British balloonist Charles Green announced that he would make his ninety-ninth ascent while riding on horseback. The nineteenth century public could not wait to see such a spectacle and, on 29 July 1828 at 5 o'clock in the morning, an immense crowd gathered outside of the Eagle Tavern in City Road, London. Spectators filled all of Old Street and City Road, even standing atop nearby buildings, all vying for the first glimpse of the famous aeronaut on his steed. The 2 August edition of the *Edinburgh Evening Courant* reports:

'For a long time the spectators, some of whom had assembled at a very early hour, were lost in conjecturing what Mr Green meant in announcing an ascent on horseback, till they were at length shewn a very pretty Shetland pony, one of the smallest breed we ever saw.'

Contemporary accounts differ regarding the breed of the pony. Many newspapers describe him as a Welsh pony, while the most detailed 1828 article on Mr Green's balloon ascent states that he was, indeed, a Shetland pony. This pony had been 'carefully trained' by Mr Green and had already made one or two balloon ascents with him to 'such heights as the ropes would allow'.[42] Described in the *Edinburgh Evening Courant* as being 'very docile,' the pony was reportedly accustomed to climbing the stairs, lying down on the hearth-rug, and drinking tea from a cup. In addition, the pony was trained to bow to ladies and to offer its foot to gentlemen when 'commanded to salute them'.

Before take-off, Mr Green exhibited the talented little pony to the crowd. According to the *Edinburgh Evening Courant*:

'In order to show the wondering and doubting crowd that no trick was intended, the beautiful little and well-trained animal, decorated with blue satin housing, bridle and ribbands, was led round the gardens, bowing to the company, and much exciting their admiration.'

A back view of two rotund Shetland ponies and their groom at feeding time. (*Sawrey Gilpin (British, 1733–1807), Two Shetland Ponies With a Groom, 1834. Oil, watercolour, gouache, and pen in brown ink on moderately thick, rough, beige, wove paper. Yale Center for British Art, Paul Mellon Collection*)

At seven o'clock, the pony was led into a stall underneath the balloon. This stall was really nothing more than a round platform attached to the bottom of the balloon. Made of 'strong and close wicker-work' and 'covered with green cloth' it provided just enough room for the pony to stand in.[43] He was secured to the platform by straps which were fastened to his little hooves. Mr Green then mounted the pony and the balloon was set loose.

There had been a rainstorm the previous evening and, though the weather was calmer, the day was still quite breezy. As a result, the balloon at once 'soared aloft taking a southerly direction, carrying with it the man and the animal'.[44] The poor pony did not know what to make of this new experience and, quite predictably, panicked. As the *Edinburgh Evening Courant* relates:

> 'The pony evidently disliked the excursion, and plunged violently at the moment of the ascent, greatly to the terror of the spectators. What Mr Green may have felt at commencing such a journey, with such a companion, we know not; his exertions to preserve quiet and order seemed wholly to occupy him, and perhaps his fears were not equal to the spectators' apprehensions; but we never saw a neck that we thought in greater jeopardy than Mr Green's, except one that was placed in the hands of the executioner.'

Fortunately, the pony soon reconciled himself to the situation and, for the rest of the voyage, remained relatively quiet. The journey itself lasted over sixteen hours, the balloon going wherever the wind decided to take it. The 20 July edition of the *Morning Post* reports:

> 'A messenger arrived at the Eagle Tavern at half-past eleven last night, with the intelligence that Mr Green descended safe, after a very fine voyage, at Beckenham, in Kent.'

Mr Green's balloon ascent on his pony proved so popular that he sought to repeat the performance. He announced that he would do so in honour of King George IV's birthday on 12 August 1828. Unfortunately, the weather was not cooperative and the ascent had to be postponed for three days. On 15 August 1828, the *Morning Chronicle* reports that 'the ascent was finally accomplished' with 'the trifling omission of the horse part of the entertainment'.

The reporter at the *Morning Chronicle* likened the exclusion of the 'Welsh Pegasus' from the balloon ascent to the exclusion of the character of Iago from Shakespeare's *Othello*, writing:

> 'As soon as we were aware of this circumstance, it forcibly recalled to our mind the Irish mode of performing Othello, with the character of Iago omitted, under the direction of Father O'Leary, as too immoral for any stage ... so, in like manner, under the beauteous trees of White Conduit House (poplars half-grown, and beech not grown at all), we heard the faint echoes of sundry sighs and moaning for the omission of the pony ...'

Another complaint was that on this occasion, Mr Green 'sailed by deputy,' sending his son in his place.[45] But the public's response to the absence of the famous aeronaut was nothing compared to their response to the absence of his tiny steed. As the *Morning Chronicle* states rather aptly, 'The balloon, to be sure, went up; but what is a balloon without a pony?'

Balloon ascents were still fairly novel in the early nineteenth century and often attracted sizeable crowds. (*unknown artist, A Balloon Ascent near Greenwich Hospital, ca. 1800. Watercolour, pen, and ink on medium, slightly textured, cream wove paper. Yale Center for British Art, Paul Mellon Collection*)

English animal painter Edwin Henry Landseer depicts the favourite horse, dogs, and hunting hawks of HRH Prince George of Cambridge. (*Sir Edwin Henry Landseer* (*British, 1802–1873*), *Favourites, the Property of H.R.H. Prince George of Cambridge, 1834 to 1835. Oil on canvas. Yale Center for British Art, Paul Mellon Collection*)

Sporting horses and hunters were frequently painted in the field alongside sportsmen and their hunting dogs. (*Thomas Woodward (British, 1801–1852), Grey Shooting Pony, Probably the Property of Johnston King, with a Groom, 1835, Oil on canvas. Yale Center for British Art, Paul Mellon Collection*)

Chapter Sixteen

The Case of the Purloined Pet Donkey

'No tidings of the donkey were ever received, and she had long since abandoned all hope of recovering it.'

North Devon Gazette, 4 March 1856

In England, sometime about 1843, a donkey was born at the farm of the Wheatley family in Shinfield, near Reading. This donkey was so remarkably small that it was given as a pet to Farmer Wheatley's young daughter, Lydia. The much-cherished animal was christened 'Tuppy' and, according to the 8 March 1856 edition of the *Hereford Times*, matured into a creature of 'asinine beauty'. When he grew large enough, he was trained to draw his young mistress about the neighbourhood in a little chaise. The sight of Miss Wheatley and her donkey chaise excited great admiration, attracting the 'especial notice' of famed nineteenth century authoress Mary Russell Mitford and other literary types, one of whom used to borrow the chaise to drive about town.

Tuppy remained with Lydia Wheatley from the day he was foaled until 1851, the year of the Great Exhibition in London. That August, while Miss Wheatley was away in London, Farmer Wheatley made the unhappy discovery that his daughter's donkey had been stolen. Many years passed and, as the 4 March 1856 edition of the *North Devon Gazette* reports, 'No tidings of the donkey were ever received, and she had long since abandoned all hope of recovering it.'

Five years later, Miss Wheatley was all grown up and living in London. One day, in February of 1856, she was returning to her residence in Regent Street when she saw a costermonger in the road. The man, who was later identified as Henry Hollis of Drury Lane, had 'the identical long-lost animal' pulling his cart.[46] According to the 1 March 1856 edition of the *Dunstable Chronicle*:

'She knew it instantly, but controlled herself sufficiently to prevent suspicion, while contriving to get into conversation with the man about the donkey. She said it was a very pretty animal, expressed a hope that he used it well, and fed it herself with a biscuit.'

Donkeys have notoriously long memories and one can only imagine how this little fellow must have felt at the miraculous appearance of his former mistress. The *North Devon Gazette* reports that he 'knew her directly'. While the *Hereford Times* states that he 'recognized her and evinced great delight'.

Donkeys were small and sturdy, making them ideal for children to ride or drive. (*John Ferneley (British, 1782–1860), Miss Catherine Herrick with her Nieces and Nephews, the Five Elder Children of the Rev. and Mrs. Henry Palmer, 1829. Oil on canvas. Yale Center for British Art, Paul Mellon Collection*)

Miss Wheatley kept Mr Hollis engaged in conversation until a policeman came into view. When the policeman approached, she stated her case to him. The officer was not unsympathetic and, after hearing her extraordinary tale, he 'took care that both the man and the donkey should be forthcoming'.[47] Later, at Bow Street, Miss Wheatley obtained a summons against Mr Hollis requiring him to show cause as to why he refused to surrender her pet donkey.

The case was adjourned so that both parties could gather their witnesses. When it resumed, an attorney named Mr Lewis appeared for the defendant. Mr Lewis immediately attempted to discredit Miss Wheatley's identification of the donkey, arguing that only a week before a woman in another police court case had been unable to identify her own husband. How then, he seemed to ask the court, could a young lady like Miss Wheatley be trusted to accurately identify a donkey she had not seen in five years?

Miss Wheatley informed the court that she 'knew her donkey too well' to be mistaken.[48] To support her assertion, she produced several witnesses, including her father and mother, a former school friend, and a farrier who had shod Tuppy when he was just a youngster. The *North Devon Gazette* relates:

> '[The witnesses] gave ample evidence in confirmation of the complainant's statement, and clearly identified 'Tuppy' (the donkey's name) beyond doubt or cavil. They also related the foregoing incidents in the animal's

For street pedlars in London, a donkey was far less expensive to keep than a horse. (*A Costermonger and his Donkey before Derby Day, Punch, Vol. XL, 1861*)

earlier career, and his worship went out to have a personal inspection of the donkey which had been brought to the door of the court.'

Undeterred by this mounting evidence, Mr Lewis called a farrier named Mr Maude for the defence. According to the *North Devon Gazette*, Mr Maude testified that he had known the donkey for several years. He also testified that the donkey was eight years old, to which Mr Wheatley remarked that 'no one could tell a donkey's age after seven'. Mr Maude conceded that this was true, but went on to state that he had shod the donkey for another costermonger, by the name of Mr Jones, six years prior when the donkey was only two years old and 'so small that you could carry it in your arms'.

Mr Jones was then called to the stand to back up Mr Maude's assertions. He swore that he had indeed bought the donkey as a two year old in 1850 for the cost of only fifteen shillings. He claimed to have had to wait for twelve months for the donkey to be old enough to be of any use to him, testifying that he had then sold the donkey to another man who, in turn, sold it to Mr Hollis.

The judge in the case, one Mr Jardine, disbelieved the evidence of the defendant. He called into question the testimony of Mr Jones, declaring that he seriously doubted whether a costermonger would pay fifteen shillings for any animal that would not be of use to him for a year or more. As for the identification by Mr Maude, the *Dunstable Chronicle* quotes the judge as stating that:

'[Mr Maude] must be a bold man indeed to swear to a donkey from merely having shod it a few times – probably without taking any particular notice of the animal at the time.'

The judge pronounced that the donkey had not been obtained honestly and ordered it to be surrendered to Miss Wheatley immediately. As the *Hereford Times* reports:

'Tuppy was adjudged the property of Miss Wheatley, and duly delivered to her amidst the applause of an admiring crowd.'

Did Mr Hollis know that the donkey that pulled his cart through London was, in fact, stolen property? Or was he an innocent victim of someone else's perfidy? It is unclear from reports at the time. However, the *North Devon Gazette* does state that Miss Wheatley wished to make Mr Hollis some compensation for the loss of the donkey. Unfortunately for Mr Hollis, the court was not in agreement on this point. The judge refused to recommend compensation for the costermonger and the case of the purloined pet donkey was then closed.

A groom is shown exercising the royal horses in this mid–nineteenth century painting by English equine artist John Frederick Herring. (*John Frederick Herring (British, 1795–1865), Exercising the Royal Horses, between 1847 and 1855. Oil on canvas. Yale Center for British Art. Gift of Reeve & Elizabeth Boies Schley*)

Everything from the horse's teeth to the nails in his shoes is visible in this extraordinarily detailed painting by equine artist John Ferneley. (*John Ferneley (British, 1782–1860), William Massey-Stanley driving his Cabriolet in Hyde Park, 1833. Oil on canvas. Yale Center for British Art, Paul Mellon Collection*)

Chapter Seventeen

The West End Rambles of London's Piccadilly Goat

'Living as he does among the aristocracy, and in the very centre of the West End, the goat has acquired some very fastidious tastes, though he is thoroughly well-behaved.'

Newcastle Courant, 4 June 1892

Sometimes called the poor man's cow, goats in the nineteenth century were used for everything from pulling carts to providing milk. Their popularity as pets, however, was often due as much to superstition as it was to economy. For example, many believed that keeping a goat in the stable would protect horses from illness or injury. In the late nineteenth century, Mr Miller, the coachman who presided over the Piccadilly stables of Mr Alfred de Rothschild, kept a goat for just that reason.

The goat was ten years old and, according to the 4 June 1892 edition of the *Newcastle Courant*, had 'no particular name'. He had come to live at Mr de Rothschild's stable in Brick Street, Piccadilly when he was only a few months old and was quite a popular figure in the neighbourhood. He was regularly noticed by 'prominent people' and even the Duke of Cambridge is reported to have stopped to 'give him a friendly tap or word'.

It was the goat's habit to go to the stable door each morning and check the weather. He was fastidious in

A sketch of the Piccadilly Goat.
(*Illustration from* The Great Streets of the World *by Richard Harding Davis, 1892*)

THE PICCADILLY GOAT.

this regard, refusing to venture out unless the day was warm and clear. As the *Newcastle Courant* reports:

'It is most amusing to see the goat come to the door at an early hour in the morning and take a careful survey in all directions; if the atmospherical and meteorological conditions do not suit its fancy it turns back and gives up outdoor exercise for the day. Should the morning prove satisfactory, the goat will walk off, and perhaps not be seen again until nightfall.'

The goat's weather predictions were well known in Piccadilly, many having observed that if he chose to leave the stable in the morning, the day was 'sure to be a fine one'. Or, as the 28 August 1894 edition of the *Belfast News-Letter* puts it, 'The Piccadilly goat was more to be relied upon as regards the weather than the best barometer.'

The goat's rambles took him from Piccadilly to Oxford Street, Regent Street and beyond. He had many friends along the way who would coax him into their shops and offer him his favourite treats, including cakes and sweetmeats. He even visited the private homes of the well-to-do. According to the *Newcastle Courant*:

'The goat has his regular houses of call in the principal West End squares and knows exactly the time of day to call when the most toothsome morsels are to be had. He is very particular in his tastes, and will accept nothing unless it be exactly what he likes.'

The goat's favourite address was that of the Duke of Cambridge. The 1 September 1890 edition of the *St. James's Gazette* reports that he could be seen there at almost any hour of the day and was a great favourite of the residents, who would allow him to 'lounge full length across the footway'. He was so popular that, while he remained in front of the Duke of Cambridge's house, the police protected his 'ample beard' from the indignity of being pulled by mischief-makers. The *St. James's Gazette* states:

'There he stands, or sits, and maintains a benevolent neutrality, in season and out of season, towards the thousands who make way for him or give him an admiring glance of regard.'

The goat has been described as being a very large, grey he-goat and 'one of the finest of his kind'.[49] But despite the praise heaped upon him, the Piccadilly goat was not without his vices. Accustomed to receiving handouts from his many friends, he did not take rejection kindly on those occasions he was refused his treats. One elderly woman in the park peddling apples and sweets out of a stall was not as generous toward the goat as he had come to expect and, as the *Belfast News-Letter* relates:

> 'One day the sight of the mounted policeman that precedes the Princess of Wales when she drives in the park passed down Piccadilly, and the old woman rose from her seat and rushed to the edge of the kerb to have a sight of Royalty. The goat improved the opportunity to resent his grievances. He walked gravely up to the stall, put his head under the board, and turned the whole stock-in-trade into the mud. Then he scampered home as fast as his legs would carry him.'

In addition to occasional bouts of mischief, and what the *Belfast News-Letter* refers to as 'tricks on some passer-by,' the goat's vices included a particular

A drawing of a goat by eighteenth century British portraitist Thomas Gainsborough. (*Thomas Gainsborough RA (British, 1727–1788), Study of a Goat, late 1770s. Black chalk and stumping, and white chalk on medium, moderately textured, beige wove paper, laid down on card. Yale Center for British Art, Paul Mellon Collection*)

fondness for tobacco. But even in this his discerning taste was evident. The *Newcastle Courant* reports, 'He will only accept a certain kind of light-coloured, mild-flavoured cigarette tobacco, to which he is rather partial.'

As of 1893, Mr Miller had had charge of the de Rothschild's stable in Piccadilly for twenty-five years. During the whole of that time, he had always kept a goat in among the horses. He had great faith in the old superstitions and believed that it was because of the goat that the de Rothschild's stable had remained free from infectious diseases. In fact, the *Newcastle Courant* reports that during an epidemic of influenza in the West End stables earlier that year, the stable housing the goat was one of the only residences untouched by illness.

Though he was impervious to disease, the Piccadilly goat was not immortal. He died in 1893 of natural causes, leading the *Belfast News-Letter* to report merely that 'his time had come, which no one could dispute'. Not only did his death affect those who had met him personally as he strolled about the city, it also impacted the town residents who, every August, were accustomed to writing to their absent friends, 'I have no news. I have not seen a face I knew since you left but the Piccadilly Goat. We share the West End together.'[50]

Blue & Yellow Maccaw

Parrots were often kept as pets during the eighteenth and nineteenth centuries. (*unknown artist, nineteenth century, Blue & Yellow Maccaw, 1832. Watercolour, with pen, in gray ink, graphite, black crayon, yellow crayon, and guoache on moderately thick, smooth, beige wove paper,. Yale Center for British Art. Gift of Donald C. Gallup, Yale BA 1934*)

Part IV

Birds

Chapter Eighteen

The Parrot, The Monkey, and the Two Rival Lovers of Madame de Choiseul

'Her caresses were distributed equally to the animals, and her thanks to the donors.'

Letter from Horace Walpole, 10 February 1786

In the late eighteenth century, Horace Walpole and his dear friend Lady Ossory corresponded on more than just the health and well-being of Tonton. They also shared the latest gossip at court and relayed humorous stories about their various friends and acquaintances. One such letter, sent on 10 February 1786, contained an entertaining anecdote about the two rival lovers of their mutual acquaintance, Françoise-Thérèse de Choiseul-Stainville. Madame de Choiseul was the daughter of French nobleman Jacques Philippe de Choiseul-Stainville. Described as a 'high-hearted' young lady, she was being pursued by both Monsieur de Coigny and Prince Joseph of Monaco.[51] Both were anxious to win her affections and each was very jealous of the other.

According to Walpole's letter, Madame de Choiseul longed for a pet parrot that would be 'a miracle of eloquence'. Such a creature was not difficult to obtain as, at the time, there were an abundance of shops in Paris which sold macaws, parrots, cockatoos and the like. One of Madame's lovers swiftly took himself off to just such a pet shop, where he obtained for his beloved the desired bird.

However, Walpole writes that Madame de Choiseul 'had two passions as well as two lovers'. In addition to desiring an eloquent parrot, she had also become enamoured of General Jackoo, a famous performing chimpanzee at Astley's Amphitheatre in London. Her second lover attempted to purchase General Jackoo from Philip Astley, the owner of the circus, but the sum Astley demanded was far too high. Madame's lover immediately went in search of a comparable monkey which he might present to his lady. As Walpole relates:

'[He] fortunately heard of another miracle of parts of the Monomotapan race, who was not in so exalted a sphere of life, being only a marmiton in a kitchen, where he had learnt to pluck fowls with an inimitable dexterity.'

An eighteenth century pastel portrait of a fashionable young lady with her pet monkey by Venetian portraitist Rosalba Carriera. (*Rosalba Giovanna Carriera (Italian, (1675–1757), Girl holding a monkey, ca. 1721. Pastel. Louvre, Paris © MEPL / Bridgeman Images*)

This monkey was not as costly as General Jackoo and the second lover easily negotiated his purchase. He presented the monkey to a delighted Madame de Choiseul, who promptly christened this new pet General Jackoo II. Walpole writes that, 'Her caresses were distributed equally to the animals, and her thanks to the donors.'

The first time Madame de Choiseul left the house, her pet parrot and her pet monkey were locked up together in her bedchamber. When she returned, Jackoo II came to greet her, but her parrot was nowhere to be found. After a search, the poor bird was at last discovered hiding under the bed, 'shivering and cowering – and without a feather, as stark as any Christian.' Apparently, Jackoo II had thought the parrot no different than the fowls he had plucked while employed as a kitchen assistant. No sooner had Madame de Choiseul shut the door, leaving the two animals alone together, than the monkey had seized the parrot and proceeded to pluck him completely bare.

On learning of this unfortunate episode, the first lover concluded that the second had given Madame the feather-plucking monkey with just such a result in mind. He challenged his rival to a duel. They fought and both were wounded. According to Walpole, 'an heroic adventure it was!'

Madame de Choiseul married Prince Joseph of Monaco in 1782. She met the guillotine in 1794, executed only one day before the fall of Robespierre at the end of the Reign of Terror. The ultimate fate of the parrot and the monkey is unknown.

Chapter Nineteen

The Widower Swan of the Château de Malmaison

'Neither time nor the snow-white charms of his new companion have had the least effect on the pride of the sable monarch; he turns from her with disgust, will not suffer her to approach him, and prefers living in perpetual widowhood to forming a Mesalliance.'

Morning Post, 1 November 1824

In the early nineteenth century, the beautiful Château de Malmaison in Paris was the home of Napoleon Bonaparte and his wife, Joséphine. It was also home to a large collection of rare and exotic animals, all of which roamed free in the gardens. Some of these animals had come to Malmaison as diplomatic gifts. Others were the result of Captain Nicolas Baudin's natural history expedition to Australia in 1800 during which French zoologists and botanists gathered native flora and fauna to bring back to France.

Amongst the native Australian creatures transported on the return voyage to France in 1803 were two black swans. Unlike many of the animals who perished during the journey, the black swans acclimatised themselves with relative ease, both on the ship and, later, in the gardens of Malmaison. There, they sailed with majestic splendour in the central lake and strutted proudly along the bank.

The French had never seen their like before. Indeed, with their deep black plumage, white wingtips, and red beaks, the black swans were widely considered 'a proverbial rarity, so improbable as almost to be deemed impossible'.[52] They were smaller than white swans, more elegant, and had a far more pleasing call than their white counterparts. According to one contemporary observer, 'Its appearance is very majestick, it is quick sighted, and has a soft, plaintive note, rather agreeable to the ear.'[53]

At Malmaison, the black swan reproduced for the first time in captivity. Swans mate for life and show exceptional care toward their young (called cygnets), fiercely protecting them from predators. At night, the cygnets sleep under the mother's wing and, during the day, if they have grown tired or cold or if the water is too deep or the waves too treacherous they often ride on the mother's back as she sails through the water. The father keeps a constant guard, both before and

Napoleon and Hortense de Beauharnais (Josephine's daughter) beside the lake at the Château de Malmaison. (*Last Residence of Napoleon at Malmaison, nineteenth century. Engraving*)

after the hatchlings emerge from the nest, ever watchful lest some harm come to his family.

Swans in general are extraordinarily long lived, with some accounts documenting a lifespan as long as thirty years. Black swans are no different. Those at the Château de Malmaison outlived the Empress Joséphine. At the time of her death in 1814, there were seven black swans still remaining in the garden. Some of these went to the Museum of Natural History and some went to Prince Eugène at Munich. Eventually, only one pair of black swans was left. It is not entirely clear from historical records, but it is possible that this remaining couple may have been the original pair that had come from Australia in 1803.

Sometime later, the female of the pair died. In an attempt to console the grieving widower, 'the most beautiful white female swan that could be procured' was brought to Malmaison and put into the canal.[54] The widower swan was far from pleased. His subsequent rejection of the white swan has been recorded in countless newspapers and magazines of the early to mid-nineteenth century. According to one account given in an 1833 issue of the *Magazine of Natural History and Journal of Zoology*:

> 'He would not be comforted: her embraces revolted his pride, he considered it would be a mésalliance to consort with a being on whom nature had not lavished the beauty of sable plumes.'

The gardener at the Château de Malmaison reported that the black swan would not tolerate the white swan 'to even approach him, or come into his sight'. She was later found at the turn of the canal, more than two hundred yards away from 'the mate who despised her snowy charms'.

The passage of time did not soften the widower swan's heart. The writer of the piece for the *Magazine of Natural History* returned to Malmaison some years later and, as he relates:

> 'I visited Malmaison sometime afterward, and found the sable monarch still a widower, faithful to his first love, and still refusing the consolation of beauty, because her colour varied from his own. What a lesson for man!'

Several other magazines reported the same turn of events, with one writing:

A black swan with white wingtips, similar to the widower swan at the Château de Malmaison. (*Black Swan, 1849. Illustrations of British Birds and Their Eggs, Vol. VI. by H. L. Meyer*)

'Neither time nor the snow-white charms of his new companion have had the least effect on the pride of the sable monarch; he turns from her with disgust, will not suffer her to approach him, and prefers living in perpetual widowhood to forming a mésalliance.'[55]

Inevitably there were those publications that sought to turn the black swan's loyalty to his original mate into a sort of morality lesson. As one columnist concludes:

'Though they have now inhabited the same piece of water for years, he still preserves his sullen dignity, and never suffers the white swan to approach him; giving thus a valuable lesson to man, that it is possible to live in a perverted state of society without suffering our principles to be contaminated.'[56]

Beneath the romantic and moral embellishments of nineteenth century writers is simple biology. Black swans and white swans are different species. Given a choice, they rarely mate with each other. However, when no other swans of their own kind are present, black swans have been known, on occasion, to pair with a white swan and produce hybridized young. Was the black swan at Malmaison simply unwilling to accept a mate of another species? Or was he truly mourning his lost love? Like much in history, we can only guess at the answer.

Today, the Château de Malmaison is open to the public for sightseeing and even available for weddings. On a tour of the house, one might view such luxurious swan-themed furnishings as swan chairs, swan carpets, and the golden swan tent bed in which Joséphine died. As for black swans themselves, they are no longer the rarity that they were in the early 1800s. They can now be seen in zoological gardens all over the world and in the wild not only in Australia, but in small populations in the United States and England as well. Many of these beautiful creatures may even be the distant relatives of those first two swans brought to Malmaison so many years ago, descendants of the widower black swan and his long lamented spouse.

CORVUS CORAX, Linn.

J. Gould & H.C. Richter, del. et lith.   Walter, imp.

Corvus Corax, the common raven, is considered to be one of the most intelligent birds in existence. (*John Gould (1804–1881), Corvus Corax – Raven, n.d. Lithograph on wove paper. Brooklyn Museum. Gift of the Estate of Emily Winthrop Miles*)

Chapter Twenty

The Ravens Who Inspired Charles Dickens

'The raven in this story is a compound of two great originals, of whom I was, at different times, the proud possessor'

Preface to *Barnaby Rudge*, Charles Dickens, March 1849

Between 1840 and 1841, Charles Dickens published his fifth novel, Barnaby Rudge, in serial format in the short-lived weekly periodical *Master Humphrey's Clock*. It was in this novel that Dickens introduced the character of Barnaby Rudge's talkative avian companion, Grip the raven. Described as having 'acquired a degree of sagacity which rendered him famous for miles round', the fictional Grip was, in fact, a composite of two real life ravens which Dickens had owned at different periods in his lifetime.

Dickens' first raven, also named Grip, was found in London by one of his friends. He gave the raven, who was then still quite young, to Dickens as a gift. Grip was a highly intelligent bird and Dickens soon grew to be very fond of him. He fed him and petted him – considerations which Grip was known to repay by loudly proclaiming 'I am a devil! I am a devil!'[57]

In his preface to the 1849 edition of *Barnaby Rudge*, Dickens states that Grip was constantly observing those around him and improving his store of knowledge 'by study and attention in a most exemplary manner'. But Grip's intellect was not always used for good. He nipped at people's ankles, stole and buried half-pence all throughout the garden and was known, on more than one occasion, to have 'terrified a Newfoundland dog' so thoroughly that the much larger animal allowed Grip to steal his dinner from right under his nose and 'walk off unmolested'.

According to Dickens, Grip was 'rapidly rising in acquirements and virtues, when, in an evil hour, his stable was newly painted'. Grip slept in the stable, generally perching on one of the horse's backs, and he had a birds' eye view of the workers and their paint. As Dickens relates:

'He observed the workmen closely, saw that they were careful of the paint, and immediately burned to possess it. On their going to dinner he ate up all they had left behind consisting of a pound or two of white lead; and this youthful indiscretion terminated in death.'

Grip did not die immediately from ingesting the lead paint. In fact, it was not until a year later that Dickens wrote of the raven's demise in a letter to a friend. This letter, dated 12 March 1841, states that Grip had been ailing for only a few days prior. Dickens and his family suspected it was as a result of some of the lead paint that Grip had eaten the previous summer still 'lingering about his vitals'. A medical man, by the name of Mr Herring, was called in to examine the ailing raven. He prescribed 'a powerful dose of castor oil,' which seemed to help in the short term, but ultimately had no effect on easing Grip's pain.

The following morning, Grip was given some more castor oil and a small meal of warm gruel, which 'he appeared to relish'. Within another two hours, however, his health had greatly deteriorated. At half past eleven, Dickens overheard the dying raven:

> 'Talking to himself about the horse and Topping's family [Topping was the coachman], and to add some incoherent expressions which are supposed to have been either a foreboding of his approaching dissolution, or some wishes relative to the disposal of his little property: consisting chiefly of half-pence which he had buried in different parts of the garden.'[58]

" GRIP," THE LATE MR. CHARLES DICKENS'S RAVEN

An engraving of Charles Dickens' pet raven, Grip which originally appeared in an 1870 edition of the *Graphic*. (*Grip, the Late Charles Dickens' Raven, 1870. Engraving. Private Collection / © Look and Learn/Bernard Platman Antiquarian Collection/Bridgeman Images*)

A portrait of Charles Dickens. (*Charles Dickens, 1873. Portrait Gallery of Eminent Men and Women of Europe and America, Vol. II.*)

At noon, Grip rose from his deathbed, paced two or three times about the coach house, and then, according to Dickens' letter, '[He] stopped to bark, staggered, exclaimed Halloa old girl! (his favourite expression), and died.'

Dickens was deeply grieved at the loss of his pet. He was also not entirely certain that Grip had succumbed to the lingering effects of lead paint. A local butcher had been heard to threaten that he would 'do for' Grip, leading Dickens to suspect that the spiteful fellow had poisoned the poor raven out of malice. As a consequence of these suspicions, he requested that Mr Herring perform a post-mortem on Grip's body. The results of this exam are unknown. The body of Grip, however, was preserved via taxidermy. Dickens would keep the stuffed raven with him until his death, after which it was sold at auction to much public excitement for the then princely sum of £120.

While still in mourning after the death of Grip, Dickens was given a new raven by a friend in Yorkshire who had found the bird residing at a village pub. This raven was older than Grip had been and, reportedly, even more intelligent. Upon arriving at the Dickens' family abode, he promptly busied himself with a variety of avian tasks. According to Dickens:

Ravens like Grip could live as long as forty years in captivity. (*Raven, Corvus Corax, Illustrations of British Birds and Their Eggs, Vol. III by H. L. Meyer, London: Simpkin, Marshall, & Co., 1846*)

'The first act of this Sage was, to administer to the effects of his predecessor, by disinterring all the cheese and half-pence he had buried in the garden – a work of immense labour and research, to which he devoted all the energies of his mind.'[59]

After the new raven had unearthed all of Grip's buried treasure, he took himself off to the stable where 'he applied himself to the acquisition of stable language'.[60] The raven was soon so adept at mimicking the stablemen, that he would sit outside of Dickens' window and 'drive imaginary horses with great skill, all day'.[61]

Dickens was not as attached to his second raven as he had been to Grip. The feeling was quite mutual. Dickens himself admitted that, though he could not have respected his second raven more, the raven had no respect for him in return, preferring instead to attach itself to the household cook.

Like Grip, this second raven's curiosity often got the better of him, especially when it came to ingesting foreign substances. During the three years he lived as Dickens' pet, he dug out and subsequently ate the mortar in the garden wall, scraped away and ingested the putty from the glass windows and tore to pieces a wooden staircase and landing, which he then swallowed in splinters. At the end of his three years with the Dickens' family, the raven took ill. He spent his final hours in front of the kitchen fire. As Dickens relates in his preface to *Barnaby Rudge,* 'He kept his eye to the last upon the meat as it roasted, and suddenly turned over on his back with a sepulchral cry of "Cuckoo!"'

Dickens remained an animal lover all of his life, but he would never again own another raven. As for Grip and his successor, though their lives were short by raven standards, their influence in the world of literature can still be felt today. Not only did they inspire the character of Grip in *Barnaby Rudge*, they also indirectly inspired American author Edgar Allan Poe to write his famous poem *The Raven* in 1845.

While working for *Graham's Magazine* in 1842, Poe was tasked with reviewing *Barnaby Rudge*. In his review, he makes special note of Grip the raven, calling him 'intensely amusing', but observing that Dickens would have done better to have made the character more prophetic. He writes:

'Its croakings might have been prophetically heard in the course of the drama ... Each might have been distinct. Each might have differed remarkably from the other. Yet between them there might have been wrought an analogical resemblance, and, although each might have existed apart, they might have formed together a whole which would have been imperfect in the absence of either.'

Only three years later, Poe published *The Raven*, a poem in which he seems to take the advice he gave to Dickens very much to heart. It skyrocketed him to instant fame. Reviewers hailed him as a genius and New York literary society welcomed him, at last, with open arms. Today, *The Raven* is still the poem for which Poe is best remembered. Even those who have never read the piece in its entirety – or anything else Poe has ever written – can recite the famous lines 'Quoth the Raven, "Nevermore".'

A hen and her chicks peck at cherries in this 1872 painting by artist Mary Smith. (*Mary Smith (1842–1878), Picking Cherries, 1872. Oil on canvas. Courtesy of the Pennsylvania Academy of the Fine Arts, Philadelphia. Gift of Russell Smith*)

Chapter Twenty-One

A Regimental Chicken

'*There is a private soldier who owns a pet pullet, which has escaped, with its owner, all the perils of battle thus far.*'

Chester Chronicle, 27 June 1863

When one thinks of nineteenth century military mascots, a chicken is not the first animal that generally comes to mind. However, a New York regiment during the American Civil War and a British regiment during the Second Anglo–Afghan War each kept a pet chicken within their ranks. The Civil War chicken was a hen by the name of Biddy. The 27 June 1863 edition of the *Chester Chronicle* quotes a portion of a letter about her from a Union soldier in General Joseph Hooker's army, which reads:

'In one of the New York State Regiments here, there is a private soldier who owns a pet pullet, which has escaped, with its owner, all the perils of battle thus far, and which is quite an acquisition to the chicken fancier, who has carried her along with him wherever he has been since last summer.'

Biddy was the lone chicken in the regiment, but she did not seem to mind her solitude. She furnished her owner with one large egg each day and is reported to have had 'a very good time by herself'. Though an odd sort of pet, she was nonetheless a favourite amongst the soldiers. As the *Chester Chronicle* reports, 'She is a fine specimen, and is quite a pet among the "boys," who take good care of her.'

Unlike Biddy – who was more of an unofficial mascot – the pet chicken in the 51st Regiment of Foot during the Second Anglo–Afghan War was regarded as a 'regimental institution'. She was even profiled in an issue of *The Bugle*, the regimental newspaper. This profile was reprinted in the 16 August 1879 edition of the *Whitby Gazette* and begins by stating:

'There is now regularly borne in the strength of the regiment a most extraordinary pet. We have heard of pet fleas, likewise of pet spiders and snakes, but never before of a pet chicken.'

This 'regimental hen,' as she is referred to, had originally been the property of Paymaster Roberts. Like Biddy, she laid one egg daily. Unfortunately, she was very particular about where she laid it. According to the profile:

> '[She] was wont daily to lay one egg, alas! for the ingratitude of henkind, in the Adjutant's tent. Nothing could prevent her; even several flagellations at the hands of a sturdy batman left her constancy unchanged.'

Unable to stop the hen from laying her eggs in the Adjutant's tent, Captain Roberts made the wise decision to give the little hen to the Adjutant as a gift. This solution worked out to the benefit of all and, in time, the hen is reported to have become 'a regular regimental institution,' travelling with the soldiers without any mishap and 'laying her one egg daily on the line march with the greatest regularity'.[62]

Though a chicken may seem to be a purely practical animal for a nineteenth century soldier to take to war, it is clear from the reports on these two regimental chickens that they were more than mere laying hens. They were valued pets and mascots. Did they survive the wars? The American Civil War ended in 1865. The Second Anglo–Afghan War ended in 1880. It is entirely possible that Biddy and the British regimental hen went home with their respective owners and lived out the rest of their days on a peaceful farm in the countryside. Regrettably, there seems to be no evidence on the ultimate fate of either of them.

A nineteenth century farmyard with a cow, a pig, a rooster, and a hen like Biddy. (*Print made by Alfred W. Cooper (British, active 1850–1901), The Farmyard, n.d. Wood-engraving with hand coloring on moderately thick, slightly textured, cream wove paper. Yale Center for British Art, Paul Mellon Collection*)

Wild rabbits and hares were very different from the sort of domestic rabbits kept as pets.
(*Unknown artist (nineteenth century) after Philip Reinagle (British, 1749–1833), Two Hares: On a Hillside, ca. 1805. Enamel on porcelain. Yale Center for British Art, Paul Mellon Collection*)

Part V

Rabbits and Rodents

PLATE.XL.

MUS LEUCOPUS, RAFF.
WHITE FOOTED MOUSE.

Three white-footed mice are portrayed in a landscape in this nineteenth century lithograph by American naturalist John James Audubon. (*John James Audubon* (*American, 1785–1851*), *White-Footed Mouse, n.d. Lithograph. Brooklyn Museum. Gift of the Estate of Emily Winthrop Miles*)

Chapter Twenty Two

Robert Burns and the Mouse at Mossgiel Farm

'*The best-laid schemes o' mice and men Gang aft a-gley.*'

To a Mouse Robert Burns, 1785

In the present day, the phrase 'of mice and men' calls up images of John Steinbeck's eponymous novella and the now legendary characters of Lennie and George. The phrase did not originate with Steinbeck, however, but with eighteenth century Scottish poet Robert Burns. In his 1785 poem *To a Mouse, on Turning Her Up in Her Nest with the Plough*, Burns writes of an experience he had while ploughing the fields at Mossgiel Farm in the parish of Mauchline, East Ayrshire.

Robert Burns and his brother, Gilbert, had removed to Mossgiel upon the death of their father in 1784. They worked the farm in order to provide for their widowed mother and five younger siblings who still remained at home. Burns took the role of peasant farmer seriously. In preparation, he read books on agriculture and cultivating crops. But Burns would never be a strictly ordinary farmer. Even as he toiled the earth at Mossgiel, his thoughts were consumed by poetry. Verses composed while out of doors working the land were transcribed each evening when he returned to the farmhouse and, according to an 1859 biography:

'At Mossgiel were rapidly produced a large proportion of those genuine native strains by which his fame was earned, and in which is specially

An 1830 mezzotint of Scottish national poet Robert Burns. (*Samuel Cousins, (1801–1887), after Alexander Nasmyth, (British, 1758–1840), Robert Burns, 1830. Yale Center for British Art, Paul Mellon Collection.*)

unfolded the most original trait of his genius – a feature almost new to poetry in general, that has especially influenced our literature through Wordsworth and his school. We mean, above all, its sympathetic tenderness for dumb life or obscure beauty in nature and the lower creatures, as sharers and companions in human emotion.'[63]

This sympathetic tenderness was never more evident than in the reaction Burns had upon turning up the nest of a little field mouse with his plough. Burns ploughed with four horses, a method which required an assistant, called a gaudsman, to drive the horses whilst Burns himself held and guided the plough. On this particular day, his gaudsman was a young man named John Blane. When the field mouse scurried from her decimated home, Blane ran after her to kill her. Burns called him back, forbidding him to harm the small, frightened creature.

After the incident, Burns became 'thoughtful and abstracted'.[64] A short while later, he read a new poem to Blane about the mouse whose nest they had inadvertently destroyed. This poem, composed as he stood beside the plough, was titled *To a Mouse, on Turning Her Up in Her Nest with the Plough*:

> Wee, sleekit, cow'rin, tim'rous beastie,
> Oh, what a panic's in thy breastie!
> Thou needna start awa sae hasty
> Wi' bickering brattle!
> I wad be laith to rin and chase thee
> Wi' murd'ring pattle.
>
> I'm truly sorry man's dominion
> Has broken nature's social union,
> And justifies that ill opinion,
> Which makes thee startle
> At me, thy poor earth-born companion,
> And fellow-mortal!
>
> I doubt na whyles, but thou may thieve;
> What then? poor beastie, thou maun live!
> A daimen icker in a thrave
> 'S a sma' request:
> I'll get a blessin' wi' the laive,
> And never miss't.
>
> Thy wee bit housie, too, in ruin!
> Its silly wa's the win's are strewin"!

And naething now to big a new ane
O, foggage green,
And bleak December's winds ensuin'
Baith snell and keen!

Thou saw the fields laid bare and waste,
And weary winter coming fast,
And cozie here, beneath the blast,
Thou thought to dwell,
Till crash! the cruel coulter passed
Out through thy cell.

That wee bit heap o' leaves and stibble,
Has cost thee mony a weary nibble!
Now thou's turned out for a' thy trouble,
But house or hald,
To thole the winter's sleety dribble,
And cranreuch cauld!

But, mousie, thou art no thy lane;
Improving foresight may be vain;
The best-laid schemes o' mice and men
Gang aft a-gley,
And lea'e us nought but grief and pain
For promised joy.

Still thou art blest, compared wi' me!
The present only toucheth thee;
But, och! I backward cast my e'e,
On prospects drear!
And forward, though I canna see,
I guess and fear.

The years that Robert Burns spent at Mossgiel Farm are generally considered to be the 'most brilliant period of poetic development' in his career.[65] Not only did he write *To a Mouse*, he also wrote *The Twa Dogs*; *To a Mountain Daisy*; *The Jolly Beggars* and many other poems, as well as some of his best-known love songs. Today, Mossgiel is a working, privately owned farm. As for the field mice who inhabit it, one can only hope that amongst their numbers are a few descendants of the *tim'rous beastie* unearthed by Robert Burns so long ago.

Domestic rabbits, like the one shown in this painting by John Hoppner, were considered to be good pets for children in the eighteenth and nineteenth centuries. (*John Hoppner RA (British, 1758–1810), Girl with a Rabbit, about 1800. Oil on canvas. Courtesy of Städel Museum/ ARTOTHEK*)

Chapter Twenty-Three

The Portable Pet Rabbit

*'No animal is a greater favourite with young folks than the Tame Rabbit, which
has long held a high place among our domestic pets.'*

Pet's Pastime, 1887

One would not know it from the countless Regency and Victorian era publications which offer advice on hunting rabbits or raising rabbits for food, but domestic rabbits were quite common as pets in the nineteenth century. Historical newspaper articles abound reporting court cases involving the theft of pet rabbits or compensation sought when a careless neighbour's dog or cat had hastened a beloved pet rabbit's demise. These pet rabbits were generally described as docile, gentle and sweet. Their disposition as placid little pets was so ubiquitous that, in some nineteenth century stories, you can find characters described as having a temperament 'as gentle as a pet rabbit'.[66] An 1895 newspaper article on choosing a wife even goes so far as to state:

'If your conception of happiness is having something pretty and innocent and troublesome about you, something that you can cherish and make happy, a pet rabbit is in every way preferable [to a wife]'[67]

Of course, the nineteenth century rabbits that most of us are familiar with are the ones that exist in classic children's literature. There is the White Rabbit in Lewis Carroll's 1865 novel *Alice's Adventures in Wonderland* and Peter Rabbit and Benjamin Bunny in the Beatrix Potter books published at the turn of the twentieth century. However, these are not the only rabbits in nineteenth century literature. Pet rabbits feature heavily in many children's books, especially during the Victorian era. One particular book from 1873 is titled *Snowdrop; or The Adventures of a White Rabbit*. It is told from Snowdrop's point of view, with the anthropomorphized rabbit recounting his life from the day of his birth in a rabbit hutch at an exclusive girls' boarding school to his ultimate retirement in the country, where he lives out the rest of his days completely at liberty.

Unlike Snowdrop, real life rabbits of the nineteenth century were not always relegated to a rabbit hutch. In fact, because of their size, rabbits were a highly portable pet. They were also usually much calmer about being transported in a basket than a cat might be. As an example, the 14 April 1875 edition of the *Shields Daily Gazette* reports the story of 'Joe the Rabbit,' a much pampered pet whose young owner decided to carry him into the city to have his photograph taken. He secured Joe in a hamper and travelled two miles to the local photography studio in town. As Joe's owner relates:

> 'When the photographer heard that he was required to take the photograph of a rabbit, he declared it was impossible, and he didn't see how it was to be done. Then he quoted the anecdote of a lady who wished to have her cat done. When the job was nearly finished, the cat sprang up the wall. I assured him that Joe would not jump up the wall. So he began to work. I sat down and took Joe on my knee.'

The photographer's concerns were not unreasonable. During the 1870s, the subject of a photograph was required to hold perfectly still for several minutes while the negative exposed. Any movement could result in the final print having a blurred appearance. But the photographer needn't have worried in Joe's case. Joe remained immobile on his owner's lap throughout the portrait session. When the photographer had finally finished his work, Joe's owner reports that:

> 'The idea of taking Joe's photograph was so novel, that the people did not know what price to charge, and in the end did not charge for Joe at all.'

In addition to being carried about town, either in a basket or in their owner's arms, pet rabbits were frequently privileged to travel greater distances – and even to accompany their owners abroad. This could sometimes lead to difficulties with local officials. A letter to the editor printed in the 1 August 1893 edition of the *London Evening Standard* relates the story of a British family travelling in Italy with their pet rabbit. The letter, written by the angry father of the family, reads in part:

> 'Early in the month, along with my wife and two children, I travelled by rail from Turin to Genoa. The fare of each was fifteen francs, and the same for baggage. My youngest child, aged thirteen, had a small pet rabbit, which she carried in a basket. En route the ticket collector happened to come to the door and espied it, and at once demanded twelve francs for its transport.'

Having only paid fifteen francs for his own ticket, the outraged father declined to pay the exorbitant rate quoted for the rabbit. The matter was then reported to the Stationmaster at Genoa who, in mockery, reduced the claim to 'eleven francs sixty centimes'. The father was ultimately obliged to pay, but this did not put an end to the matter. As he relates:

> 'By way of retaliation, the officials insisted on opening some of my baggage, perhaps thinking to find other rabbits there. But the matter did not end there. The Octroi officials, scenting their prey, demanded thirty centimes, although informed that it was a pet animal and not destined for the family pie.'

One might argue that, despite the alleged extortion perpetrated by the Italian officials, at least they allowed the rabbit to ride on the train. Thanks to the bizarre logic of a Pullman palace car porter, an American lady travelling with her pet rabbit was not so lucky. An 1884 article, published in both the British and American newspapers, reports the humorous incident:

> 'A Pullman palace car porter refused to admit a lady's pet rabbit in a car, and was shown a small turtle carried by another passenger, with the query why a rabbit was excluded and a turtle admitted. "Cats is dogs and rabbits is dogs," was his emphatic answer, "but a turtle is an insect."'[68]

The exigencies of train travel notwithstanding, rabbits remained favoured pets throughout the nineteenth century. Though they would never attain quite the same level of popularity as dogs or even cats, to those who loved them, they were as integral a part of the family as any other companion animal.

A school of sharks converge on a derelict fishing boat. (*Winslow Homer (American, 1836–1910), Sharks; also The Derelict, 1885. Watercolour over graphite on cream, moderately thick, moderately textured wove paper. Brooklyn Museum, Gift of the Estate of Helen Babbott Sanders*)

Part VI

Reptiles and Fish

Chapter Twenty-Four

The Sailor and the Shark

'No more was expected to be heard of him; but from the above Circumstances it has proved somewhat similar to the Fate of Jonas in the Belly of a Whale (young Thompson's Coffin was a living Shark,) though he was not fortunate as Jonas to escape.'

Northampton Mercury, 15 December 1787

For centuries, there have been tales of giant aquatic creatures lurking in the depths of the River Thames. Some of these tales were based on actual fact. In the eighteenth and nineteenth centuries, for example, it was not uncommon to find porpoises in the river. And once, fishermen on the Thames even encountered a small whale. Perhaps the most famous of these tales – as well as the most extraordinary – is the true story of the killer shark caught in the Thames in 1787.

On 1 January 1787, some fishermen spied a shark in the river and, with much difficulty, captured the creature and drew it into their boat. The shark was alive, but very sickly. The cause of his illness was soon discovered. Upon taking him ashore and cutting him open, the fishermen found within his body a silver watch, chain, and cornelian seal. The 15 December 1787 edition of the *Northampton Mercury* reports that they also found, 'some Pieces of Gold Lace, which were conjectured to have belonged to some young Gentleman, who was swallowed by that voracious Fish.'

On further examination, it was found that the watch was engraved with the maker's name and number: Henry Watson, London, No. 1369. Mr Watson lived in Shoreditch and, when applied to for information regarding that particular watch, the *Northampton Mercury* reports that Mr Watson revealed that he had:

'... sold the Watch two Years ago to a Mr Ephraim Thompson, of Whitechapel, as a Present for his Son on going out on his first Voyage (as what is called a Guinea-Pig) on board the ship Polly, Capt. Vane, bound to Coast and Bay.'

A guinea pig was sailor's slang for an inept or inexperienced sailor, which proved an all too apt description of young Thompson. Not far into his journey, about

A view of the Thames as it looked in the early nineteenth century. (*John Varley, (British, 1778–1842), A View along the Thames towards Chelsea Old Church, between 1810 and 1815. Oil on canvas. Yale Center for British Art, Paul Mellon Collection*)

three leagues off of Falmouth, a rainsquall descended and, as the 1787 issue of the *New Annual Register* relates, 'Master Thompson fell overboard, and was no more seen.'

After receiving the news of Thompson's death at sea, his friends and family in London expected to hear no more on the subject. One might imagine that the gruesome discovery, two years later, of Thompson's watch and clothing inside the belly of a shark would have been an unwelcome update on their lost loved one. Instead, it appears to have provided some measure of closure for Thompson's father, who promptly purchased the dead shark to display as a memorial to his son. As the *Northampton Mercury* states:

'Mr Ephraim Thompson has purchased the Shark, which he calls his Son's Executor – and the Watch, &c. which he considers as his last Legacy.'

Thompson's father also had the small satisfaction of knowing that it was likely his son's watch and clothing that had made the shark so sickly. According to the *New Annual Register*:

> 'The body and other parts, had either been digested, or otherwise voided; but the watch and gold lace not being able to pass through it, the fish had thereby become sickly, and would in all probability very soon have died.'

This incident was notable for many reasons. Not only did the shark return the belongings of its victim to London – an extraordinary event in and of itself – but it was also the largest shark on record to have ever been discovered in the Thames:

> 'From the tip of the snout to the extremity of the tail 9 feet 3 inches; from the shoulder to the extremity of the body, 6 feet 1 inch; round the body in the thickest part, 6 feet 9 inches; the width of the jaws when extended, 17 inches; it had five rows of teeth, and from that circumstance was supposed to have been five years old.'[69]

To this day, the 1787 shark remains the largest ever caught in the Thames, but it has not been the only shark. On 2 November 1891, the *Dundee Evening Telegraph* reported the story of a six-foot shark found in the Thames, writing that, 'The animal followed a Dutch ship almost the whole way from Rotterdam.'

The master of the Dutch vessel had his baby on board and was convinced that this was the reason for the shark's pursuit. Upon arriving in London, he offered a £1 reward to anyone who could capture the shark. It took several days and many

The Porbeagle shark is just one of the many varieties of shark that may have made its way into the Thames in the eighteenth and nineteenth centuries. (*Porbeagle Shark, 1862–1865. Illustration. A history of the fishes of the British Islands by Jonathan Couch*)

attempts, but in the end an 'ex-champion weight-lifter' by the name of Charles M'Kenna managed to capture the shark with a 'huge cod hook baited with beef'.

In 1898, another shark was caught in the Thames, this time in a fisherman's net. The 12 September issue of the *Morning Post* reports the shark's measurements at just under five feet in length. Not as large as the Great White in *Jaws*, certainly, but large enough to put a scare into Victorians of the era.

What kind of sharks were these? It is never mentioned in any of the accounts; however, the 1903 *Report on the Sea Fisheries and Fishing Industries on the Thames Estuary*, as prepared by Dr James Murie, describes several larger varieties of shark which might have made their way into the Thames, including the Hammerhead Shark, the Long-Tailed Thresher Shark, and the Porbeagle Shark.

It is hard to imagine just what occurred after Ephraim Thompson's son fell overboard on his first voyage out to sea. Was the shark found two years later in the Thames really the one who had killed him? Or was he merely a scavenger who had happened upon Thompson's remains? In this instance, history provides no answers, but one does not need to know every gruesome detail to appreciate that the story of the 1787 shark in the Thames is one of the most extraordinary in English animal history.

Chapter Twenty-Five

The Alligator in the Thames

'It is idle to inquire how the alligator found in the Thames crossed the Atlantic …'
Punch, 1870

In the spring of 1870, while navigating his barge up the River Thames, waterman W. Pockling of Bermondsey spotted a four-foot long alligator swimming in the water. According to the 23 April 1870 edition of the *Essex Newsman*, the alligator was 'alive, but much exhausted'. Mr Pockling managed to catch the creature and haul it into his boat. Once on shore, he engaged two young men to carry the alligator to the premises of Mr Charles Jamrach in Ratcliff Highway.

Mr Jamrach was a celebrated importer of wild beasts and other natural curiosities. He was also slightly notorious. Thirteen years prior, a Bengal tiger he had imported managed to escape from its cage. It ran off into the East End and, before it could be caught, severely mauled a ten-year-old boy. The father of the boy sued Jamrach for damages and was ultimately awarded £60 for his son's injuries.

The incident with the Bengal tiger did not deter him from importing other dangerous animals. In his menagerie in Ratcliff Highway, he proudly displayed – and offered for sale – lions, tigers, monkeys, kangaroos, zebras, exotic birds and reptiles of every variety. For a short time in 1858, he even boasted a rhinoceros. His methods of managing his menagerie were questionable, but no one could doubt his expertise when it came to identifying rare creatures.

Unfortunately for Mr Pockling, when he presented the alligator he had found in the Thames to Mr Jamrach, he did not respond with an appropriate identification. Instead, he claimed that the alligator belonged to him. But that was not all. According to Jamrach, the alligator was not even an alligator. As the 20 April 1870 edition of the *Morning Post* reports: 'Mr Jamrach said the reptile brought to him was not an alligator, but a lizard, which had escaped from his premises a few days previous.'

Mr Pockling did not believe that the creature he had found in the Thames was an escapee from the menagerie. Nor did he believe that the creature was anything other than an alligator. Unwilling to relinquish his claim, he went straight to the

THE ALLIGATOR,
In the Gardens of the Zoological Society.

London, Thomas Kelly

A nineteenth century alligator kept in the gardens of the Zoological Society of London. (*The Alligator in the Gardens of the Zoological Society of London, nineteenth century. Etching with watercolour. Wellcome Library, London. Creative Commons Attribution 4.0 International Public License*)

Thames Police Court and brought a complaint against Jamrach, accusing him of unlawfully detaining his alligator.

Upon hearing the evidence, the magistrate declared that Mr Jamrach had 'no right whatever to detain the alligator'.[70] He stated that he would send a policeman round to speak with him and, if the alligator was not promptly restored to Mr Pockling, he would then issue a summons. At this point, Jamrach had not yet been interviewed. When the police-constable arrived in Ratcliff Highway to speak with him, the *Morning Post* reports that Jamrach reiterated that the alligator was a lizard that had escaped from his collection, stating that:

'[He] believed the reptile found its way into the London Dock, about 300 yards from his own menagerie and collection, and made its way through one of the locks into the river.'

Mr Jamrach went on to tell the police-constable that the lizard had been exhausted upon its arrival back at his shop. In order to revive it, he had put it into a warm bath and then wrapped it up in flannels and placed it in front of the fire. When it had thoroughly recovered from its ordeal, he sent it to the Zoological Gardens, but, as he told the police-constable, 'He was very willing to send for it and bring it before the magistrate for inspection if he wished.'

In the end, Mr Jamrach and the lizard did not have to appear in front of the magistrate. Though Mr Pockling continued to insist that the lizard was an alligator, after listening to the police-constable's report, the magistrate came to the conclusion that Mr Jamrach was much more qualified to identify the creature than Mr Pockling. He refused to grant a summons in the case, leaving Mr Pockling to seek his remedy in County Court.

In the meanwhile, the strange case of the alligator in the Thames had sparked a great deal of public interest. Newspapers and magazines of the day speculated as to where the alligator might have come from. The 21 April 1870 issue of the *Southern Reporter* suggests that the alligator had been brought to England 'as a curiosity' and, after making its escape, had been too exhausted by the Thames water to go any further. While an article on the alligator in an 1870 issue of *Punch* declares that the origin of the alligator is of little matter, stating:

'It is idle to inquire how the alligator found in the Thames crossed the Atlantic or to speculate on the probability that it escaped from some vessel importing it for Mr Jamrach, or for the Zoological Society. We may, however, exercise our rational faculties perhaps to advantage, by considering whether, if we should be surprised at the appearance of an alligator in the Thames, there may not have been equal reason for surprise to those who saw the first crocodile that appeared in the Nile?'

All too soon, the enquiring public would learn, much to their disappointment, that Mr Jamrach had been telling the truth all along. The alligator found in the Thames was, in fact, a 'Lacerta' or lizard. This appears to have closed the case for Mr Pockling and Mr Jamrach, but the 1870 incident of the alligator in the Thames was not the only time a crocodile or alligator was reported to have appeared in the river. On 21 October 1836, the *Royal Cornwall Gazette* related the story of a man who, while steering his barge along the Thames, 'observed a black motionless object in the water'. As the newspaper reports:

'Upon his attempting to draw it out, [it] moved, and his hand was immediately severely lacerated; he, however, succeeded in getting it into the barge, when, to his great astonishment, it proved to be a young alligator. It was purchased for and removed to the Surrey Zoological Gardens.'

Another incident occurred in the summer of 1897, during which a crocodile managed to live in the Thames for over a month. This crocodile was a fugitive from the grounds of Mr D'Oyly Carte's estate at Weybridge. After making its escape, the 12 July 1897 edition of the *Exeter and Plymouth Gazette* reports that the crocodile made its way into the river 'where for some time it was seen disporting itself'. Anxious to be reunited with his exotic pet, Mr D'Oyly Carte offered a reward for its capture and return. However, as the newspaper states, 'The crocodile eluded the efforts of those who endeavoured to catch it.'

After a month during which the crocodile could regularly be seen swimming in the Thames, Mr D'Oyly Carte increased the amount of the reward. This was enough incentive for some local watermen to make a thorough search for the crocodile. After a time, they were able to catch the elusive creature in their net and return it to its master. The 16 July 1897 issue of the *Western Gazette* reports that the crocodile was, 'None the worse for its month's stay in the river.'

An illustration of a Victorian man being chased by a large alligator. (*Chased by an Alligator, 1883. Illustration. Reptiles and Birds: A Popular Account of Their Various Orders, with a Description of the Habits and Economy of the Most Interesting by Louis Figuier*)

Today, Thames water is generally considered too chilly to support crocodiles or alligators for any length of time. Nevertheless, there are still occasional reports of them swimming in the river or basking on the bank. Most of these reports have been proven false, but if history is anything to judge by, one should never discount such tales completely.

A study of a red fox by Swiss animal painter Jacques-Laurent Agasse, 1810–1830. (*Jacques-Laurent Agasse (Swiss, 1767–1849), Study of a Fox, 1810–1830. Oil on paper laid to board. Yale Center for British Art, Paul Mellon Collection*)

Part VII

Strange and Exotic Pets

Chapter Twenty-Six

The Duke of Richmond's Pet Fox and Viscount Doneraile's Vixen

'His Grace seemed much pleased, and expressed something like a wish the fox should be purchased.'

The *Gentleman's Magazine*, 1819

A fox was not a common pet in either the eighteenth or the nineteenth century. Nevertheless, both Charles Lennox, 4th Duke of Richmond, and Hayes St. Leger, 4th Viscount Doneraile, kept pet foxes for a time. This unconventional choice of animal companion would not end well for either of them. The duke died in 1819. The viscount died in 1887. Each met his painful end as a result of a bite from his pet fox.

The Duke of Richmond died in Ontario on 28 August 1819. Early newspaper reports in England claimed that the duke had taken ill as a result of great fatigue and having suffered wet feet during his travels. Later reports confirmed that the duke had, in fact, died as a result of hydrophobia, or rabies, contracted when he was bitten by his pet fox.

The duke's pet fox was a fairly new acquisition. While on a tour of what was then called 'the Canadas,' he was walking about a local village, accompanied by his dog, Blucher, when Blucher spied a fox lingering nearby. The fox appeared to be quite friendly and, after a short time, Blucher and the fox began to play together. An excerpt from a private letter published in the 1819 issue of the *Gentleman's Magazine* explains that, upon seeing his dog engaged in play with the fox, 'His Grace seemed much pleased, and expressed something like a wish the fox should be purchased.'

Having heard the duke express a desire to have the fox, a servant made arrangements to purchase the fox that same night. The next morning, the letter reports that Sir Charles Saxton found the fox tied in front of a servant's tent, appearing to be 'much irritated from his restrained situation under a scorching sun'. Sir Charles requested that the servant move the fox to a shadier location. The fox was then taken to the duke's residence, where it was tied to a gate in front of the house.

On leaving his house that morning, the duke at once observed the fox tied outside and, recognizing him from the previous day, he approached him and

An 1807 mezzotint of Charles Lennox, 4th Duke of Richmond. (*Henry Meyer (British, circa 1782–1847), Charles Lennox, 4th Duke of Richmond, 1807. Mezzotint. Photo © Museum Associates/ LACMA*)

asked 'Is this you, my little fellow?' Sir Charles attempted to prevent the duke from touching the fox, informing him that the fox was in a highly irritated state and warning him to be careful lest the little wild creature should bite him. The duke was unconcerned. He is reported to have replied 'No, no, the little fellow will not bite me.' He reached out his hand to the fox to stroke its head and, as the letter relates, 'The fox snapped and made three scratches on the back of his hand, which drew blood. His Grace, quickly drawing it back, said, "Indeed, my friend, you bite very hard."'

The 30 October 1819 edition of the *Globe* reports that, by the next morning, the Duke of Richmond was experiencing 'an uneasy sensation in his shoulder'. However, no other symptoms presented themselves until the duke returned from his tour at the end of August. At that time, he reported a 'strange sensation' when drinking a glass of wine and water. A local surgeon was called that same night to bleed him. The duke felt so much better after being bled that the next morning he went out for a long walk in the woods. It was during this walk, that he first began to exhibit an unnatural aversion toward water. The 27 October 1819 edition of the *Morning Chronicle* states:

'At the sight of some stagnant water, his Grace hastily leaped over a fence, and rushed into an adjoining barn, whither his dismayed companions eagerly followed him.'

This aversion to water only increased. According to the letter in the *Gentleman's Magazine*, the duke became irritable whenever he must cross even 'the smallest streamlets in the woods' and, on one occasion, 'he ran from them into the woods, as if to shun the sight of water'. The disease was progressing rapidly now and, as the *Morning Chronicle* reports, 'He was with difficulty removed to a miserable hovel in the neighborhood.'

The Duke of Richmond spent his final hours in that miserable hovel being nursed by a devoted Swiss servant. He was not always in his right mind, but he did experience occasional intervals of lucidity. During one such episode, the duke dictated a letter to his daughter, Lady Mary Lennox, reminding her of an incident five months prior when he had been bitten by a favourite family dog who had later run mad. According to the *Morning Chronicle*, it was this recollection that gave the duke 'but too sure a presentiment of his approaching fate'.

He died early in the morning on 28 August 1819. The letter in the *Gentleman's Magazine* asserts that he suffered 'excruciating torments' in his final moments. While the article in the *Morning Chronicle* reports that he 'expired in the arms' of his faithful Swiss servant, a man who had remained by his side throughout the course of his short and ultimately fatal illness.

Of peculiar interest, the Duke of Richmond's death notice in the *Gentleman's Magazine* is printed right beside the death notice of Hayes St Leger, 2nd Viscount Doneraile. Sixty-eight years later in 1887, his grandson, the 4th Viscount, would also die as a result of a bite from his pet fox.

St Leger was a noted huntsman and widely considered 'one of the best authorities in the world on foxhunting'.[71] He had a tame vixen which he had raised from a cub. He would often take her up with him in his carriage when he went driving. On one occasion, as the coachman was lifting the vixen into the carriage, she bit him and then, afterwards, attacked Lord Doneraile.

He was wearing gloves when he was bitten. Nevertheless, as a precaution, he and his coachman removed to Paris to be treated by the noted scientist Louis Pasteur, who was, at the time, in the early stages of developing a rabies vaccine. Unfortunately, when they arrived, Pasteur was not at home. They waited for him and when he returned, approximately one week later, he began treating both Lord Doneraile and his coachman.

There is some dispute as to whether Lord Doneraile completed his course of treatment with Pasteur. According to some reports, he grew bored and returned home to Doneraile Court, the family seat in County Cork, Ireland. Other sources state that he had been fully treated before returning home and that Pasteur had pronounced him 'out of danger'.[72] In either case, the treatment appears to have been unsuccessful. The 3 September 1887 edition of the *Ballymena Observer* reports, 'M. Pasteur's treatment must have come too late, for the unfortunate nobleman became ill, and died on Friday from the effects of hydrophobia.'

He died on the morning of 26 August at Doneraile Court in Ireland. Newspapers of the day reported the cause of death as hydrophobia. As for the fox itself, Lady Doneraile sent it to a local veterinary surgeon for observation. After two days in residence, it died as a result of its illness. A post mortem examination was later conducted, confirming that the fox had indeed been mad.

Chapter Twenty-Seven

A Victorian Flea Circus

'The public believed, and no doubt believe to this day, that the fleas were really tamed and taught; and I have heard sensible people gravely bring forward the exhibition of the "Industrious Fleas" as an instance of what ingenuity and patience can accomplish.'

Notes and Queries, 1858

D uring the nineteenth century, the flea circus was a popular sideshow attraction. Often billed as the 'smallest circus in the world,' it took place in a ring the size of a common dinner plate and consisted of fleas performing various circus stunts, such as juggling and tightrope walking. Circus fleas were alleged to be of remarkable intelligence. This was, of course, not entirely the case. The performance put on by the fleas owed far more to the showmanship of the flea circus proprietor than it did to any intelligence of the fleas themselves.

Nevertheless, flea trainers of the day were happy to discuss their methods of flea selection and training with the Victorian press. Some even seem to have believed that fleas had moral character and intelligence which, when spotted by the astute trainer, could be translated into a solid work ethic and an impressive acrobatic display. But not every flea was considered smart enough to join the circus. An 1886 article in *St. Nicholas Magazine* explains:

'Some are exceedingly apt scholars, while others never can learn, and so it is that great numbers of fleas are experimented with before a troupe is accepted.'

After selecting what he believed to be the most intelligent fleas, the proprietor of the flea circus – who was often also the trainer – subjected the fleas to a period of rigorous training. The first step in this regime was to harness the flea by attaching a thin piece of gold wire, cord, or hair around its midsection. This was a very delicate operation, requiring a microscope or magnifying device and a pair of tweezers.

Once the flea was secured in its harness, the next stage of training could begin. This phase of training generally focused on jumping. Excessive jumping was

Fleas are depicted in period garb, driving and riding in Victorian vehicles. (*The Go-As-You-Please Race, 1899. Illustration. St. Nicholas Illustrated Magazine, Vol. 26*)

undesirable in a circus flea for several reasons, not the least of which was that an unruly flea might leap straight out of the ring, thus prematurely ending the show. Most nineteenth century flea trainers used the same method to curb a flea's desire to jump. The flea was either placed in a glass phial or under a thimble so that whenever he jumped he would bang his head against the wall. After several weeks of this treatment, the flea is reported to have abandoned his desire to jump.

With this lesson learned, the flea was ready to join his intelligent comrades in the troupe. The fleas in the troupe were trained daily until they were finally ready to perform in front of an audience. Typically, the audience at a flea circus consisted of as many humans with magnifying glasses as could fit around the stage. When they approached, the proprietor placed the circus ring on a table in front of them. The ring was bordered by a series of small boxes which housed the performers. At a word from the proprietor, the doors to these houses opened and the fleas would leap out into the ring.

What the fleas did next depended entirely on the creativity of the proprietor. In Signor Bertolotto's Exhibition of Industrious Fleas – a famous 1830s flea troupe which is reported to have performed in front of the royal families of Europe – the fleas engaged in a variety of human-like activities. There was a flea ballroom where fleas danced and played musical instruments, a flea fortune-teller, a flea duel, and various flea conveyances, including a mail coach and a tandem, in which fleas featured as both passengers and horses.

The final exhibition of the Industrious Fleas in London, 1869, boasted fleas driving locomotives, pulling a line of battleships, and toting heavy artillery.

Adding to the militaristic atmosphere of the performance were flea officers in the British Army and Navy with various vessels and weaponry under their command. According to one report:

'One flea (in the Army) fired from behind a bastion a cannon of such destructive proportions that it had killed several of his predecessors (and thus led to his own promotion), besides knocking silly other civilian fleas in the neighbourhood.'[73]

The 1880s flea circus profiled in *St. Nicholas Magazine* had a much more competitive air. It began with a flea race in which five fleas, each wearing a different colour of tissue paper, were set off to hop madly about the ring. The first flea to cross the designated finish line was deemed the winner. The next performance consisted of a flea dance. The tissue-paper clad fleas were paired into couples and again were set off to hop around the ring in relative chaos.

An advertisement for the London performance of Professor Likonti's Roumanian Flea Circus in which fleas engage in a variety of popular flea circus activities. (*Professor Likonti's Roumanian Flea Circus, 1896. Advertisement. The Strand Magazine*)

A circus flea is
depicted performing
the high wire act.
(*Signor Pulex Irritanci*
on the Tight-Rope,
1899. Illustration. St.
Nicholas Illustrated
Magazine, Vol. 26)

A hurdle race followed and then, just as in Signor Bertolotto's troupe, a large number of fleas were released into the ring, harnessed to tiny coaches with gold wire thread. There was a 'tally-ho coach' that was smaller than a pea, an 'Eskimo sled' less than a quarter inch long, and a 'trotting sulky' that appeared to be made out of hair or bristles of some sort.

What followed was another episode of flea chaos. The fleas pulling the tally-ho coach 'jumped their traces,' the flea driving the Eskimo sled was thrown out of the vehicle, and the flea pulling the sulky leapt straight up into the air, its sulky flying behind it. For several moments, there was sheer pandemonium, but the canny proprietor, with the aid of his tweezers, soon had the fleas back in order.

The grand finale of many a flea circus was the high wire act. In the 1880s flea circus, this performance featured 'Signor Pulex Irritanci,' a flea touted as being a 'world renowned tight-rope performer'. The proprietor of the circus placed two pins on the stage four inches apart, connecting them with a silver wire. Signor Irritanci was then brought out in a cut glass bottle. The proprietor deposited the famous flea onto the high wire and, as *St. Nicholas Magazine* relates:

'He boldly started out upon the wire over which his little clawed toes seemed
to fit. In the middle, and over the terrific abyss, he balanced up and down
for a second, stood upon his longest legs, and then moved on, crossing in
safety, and thus ending the circus, at least for that occasion.'

When the performance was over, the fleas were unharnessed in order to be fed. Fleas required blood for sustenance. It was provided easily enough by their trainers, many of whom allowed their circus troupe to graze freely on the back of their own arm or hand. In some cases, such as with the trainer of the Exhibition of Industrious Fleas in 1869, they fed as many as thirty-two fleas each night from their own blood.

Circus fleas enjoyed a much longer lifespan than their unemployed brethren. Though an average flea lived only 8–12 weeks, circus fleas of the Victorian era are reported to have had a lifespan of as much as eleven months. Of course, as one flea trainer points out, some died much earlier as a result of overwork or 'through a proud spirit' which would not accept captivity.[74]

The first flea circus on record was opened in 1812 by Heinrich Degeller in Stuttgart. From then until the early twentieth century, flea circuses remained a popular sideshow attraction. Most continued to employ live fleas, but as time wore on and hygiene methods improved there were not as many fleas available to recruit as performers. Eventually, some flea circuses began to use other methods, such as electricity or magnets, to move the little vehicles about the ring. This is the primary reason that so many today believe that nineteenth century flea circuses were nothing but a hoax.

Sources

ARONSON, Theo. *Napoleon and Josephine: A Love Story*. New York: St. Martin's Press, 1990.

The Art Journal, Volume 53. London: J. S. Virtue & Co., 1891.

Atalanta, Vol. V. London: Atalanta Office, 1891.

BIRCH, George Henry. *London on Thames in Bygone Days*. London: Seeley & Co., 1903.

The Bookman, Vol. XI. New York: Dodd, Mead, & Co., 1898.

BOSWELL, James. *The Life of Samuel Johnson*. London: J. M. Dent & Sons, 1791.

BOYLE, Frederick. *Memoirs of Thomas Dodd, William Upcott, and George Stubbs, R.A.* Liverpool: Joseph Mayer, 1879.

BRETON, Guy. *Napoleon and his Ladies*. New York: Coward-McCann Inc., 1965.

BURNS, Robert. *The Poetical Works and Letters of Robert Burns*. Edinburgh: Gall & Inglis, 1859.

BYRON, George Gordon. *The Works of Lord Byron in Verse and Prose, including his Letters, Journals, etc.* Hartford: Silas Andrus & Son, 1851.

CHAMBERS, Robert. Ed. *The Life and Works of Robert Burns, Vol. II*. Edinburgh: W. R. Chambers, 1856.

Correspondence of Horace Walpole with George Montagu, Esq., Vol. III. London: Henry Colburn, 1837.

The Court Magazine and Monthly Critic, Vol. X. London: John Bell, 1842.

CUNNINGHAM, Peter, ed. *The Letters of Horace Walpole, Earl of Orford, Vol. VIII & Vol. IX*. London: Henry G. Bohn, 1859.

DAVIS, Richard Harding. *The Great Streets of the World*. New York: C. Scribner's Sons, 1892.

DELANO, Amasa. *A Narrative of Voyages and Travels in the Northern and Southern Hemispheres*. Boston: E. G. House, 1817.

DUNNE, John Hart. *From Calcutta to Pekin, Being Notes Taken from the Journal of an Officer Between Those Places*. London: Sampson Low, Son, and Co., 1861.

FORSTER, John. *The Life of Charles Dickens, Vol. I*. London: Chapman & Hall, 1872.

The Gardens and Menagerie of the Zoological Society Delineated, Vol. II. Chiswick: John Sharpe, 1831.

Gentleman's Magazine and Historical Chronicle, Vol. LXXXIX. London: John Nichols and Son, 1819.

GASKELL, Elizabeth. *The Life of Charlotte Brontë, Vol. I & II*. London: Smith, Elder, and Co., 1857.

Graham's Lady's and Gentleman's Magazine, Vol. XX. Philadelphia: George R. Graham, 1842.

HALL, Henry Foljambe. *Napoleon's Letters to Josephine, 1796–1812*. London: J. M. Dent and Co., 1901.

Harper's Weekly, Vol. XV. New York: Living History Incorporated, 1871.

HOEY, Brian. *Pets by Royal Appointment*. London: The Robson Press, 2014.

JESSE, George Richard. *Researches Into the History of the British Dog: From Ancient Laws, Charters, and Historical Records, Vol. I & II*. London: Robert Hardwicke, 1866.

KEIM, Albert and LUMET, Louis. *Charles Dickens*. New York: Frederick A. Stokes Company, 1914.

KNAPTON, Ernest John. *Empress Josephine*. London: Penguin, 1969.

KNOX, Thomas Wallace. *Dog Stories and Dog Lore*. New York: Cassell & Co., 1887.

The Lancet, Vol. I. London: John James Croft, 1887.

The Leisure Hour, Vol. VII. London: William Stevens, 1858.

Letters of Queen Victoria: A Selection from Her Majesty's Correspondence Between the Years 1837 and 1861. London: John Murray, 1908.

LEVY, Arthur. *The Private Life of Napoleon. Vol. I*. New York: Scribner and Sons, 1894.

Lippincott's Monthly Magazine, Vol. X. London: J. B. Lippincott, 1872.

The Literary Gazette and Journal of Belles Lettres, Arts, Sciences, no. 102–153. London: H. Colburn, 1819.

Littell's Living Age, Vol. XIX. Boston: Littell, Son and Co., 1857.

Littell's Living Age, Sixth Series, Vol. VII. Boston: T. H. Carter & Company, 1895.

MACK, Maynard. *Alexander Pope: A Life*. New York: W. W. Norton & Co., 1986.

The Magazine of Natural History and Journal of Zoology, Botany, Mineralogy, Geology, and Meteorology, Vol. VI. London: Longman, Rees, Orme, Brown, Green, and Longman, 1833.

MCLYNN, Frank. *Napoleon: A Biography*. New York: Arcade Publishing, 1997.

MERRILL, Arthur Lawrence. *Life and Times of Queen Victoria Containing a Full Account of the Most Illustrious Reign of Any Sovereign in the History of the World*. Philadelphia: World Bible House, 1901.

The Minerva, Or: Literary, Entertaining, and Scientific Journal, Vol. I. New York: J. Seymour Press, 1824.

MOORE, Thomas. *Letters and Journals of Lord Byron*. Paris: Baudry's European Library, 1833.

Motography, Vol. V. Chicago: Electricity Magazine Corporation, 1911.

MURIE, James. *Report on the Sea Fisheries and Fishing Industries on the Thames Estuary, Part 1*. London: Waterlow Bros., 1903.

Notes and Queries, Vol. V. London: Bell & Daldy, 1858.

Once a Week: An Illustrated Miscellany of Literature, Art, Science, & Popular Information, Volume IX. London: Bradbury & Evans, 1863.

PAULL, Mrs. Henry H. B. *Only a Cat; or The Autobiography of Tom Blackman*. London: George Routledge & Sons, 1877.

Pearson's Magazine, Vol. 5. London: C. Arthur Pearson Ltd., 1898.

Pet's Pastime: Illustrated Stories in Prose and Verse. London: George Routledge and Sons, 1887.

PIOZZI, Hester Lynch. *Anecdotes of Samuel Johnson, LL.D. During the Last Twenty Years of His Life.* London: T. and J. Allman, 1826.

PIOZZI, Hester Lynch. *Letters to and from the late Samuel Johnson, LL.D, Vol. II.* London: A. Strahan and T. Cadell, 1788.

POPE, Alexander, and BUTT, John Everett *The Poems of Alexander Pope: A One-volume Edition of the Twickenham Text with Selected Annotations.* New Haven: Yale U, 1963.

POPE, Alexander, et al. *The Works of Alexander Pope: Correspondence, Vol. IX.* London: J. Murray, 1871.

POPE, Alexander. *The Works of Alexander Pope, Vol. II.* London: J. F. Dove, 1822.

The Portfolio, Vol. IV. London: William Charlton Wright, p. 1825.

Punch, Vol. 58–59. London: Punch Publications Ltd., 1870.

ROBINSON, Agnes Mary Frances. *Emily Brontë.* London: W. H. Allen, 1883.

Scribner's Monthly, Vol. II. New York: Scriber & Co., 1871.

Some Scarborough Faces Past and Present. Scarborough: Scarborough Gazette Printing and Publishing, 1901.

SPENCE, Joseph. *Observations, Anecdotes, and Characters of Books and Men.* London: John Murray, 1820.

Sporting Magazine, Vol. 19. London: J. Wheble, 1803.

St. Nicolas Illustrated Magazine, Vol. XIII. New York: Century Co., 1886.

STANHOPE, Philip Dormer, 4th Earl of Chesterfield. *Lord Chesterfield's Letters to his Son in Three Volumes, Vol. I.* London: J. Walker, 1810.

STEPHEN, Leslie. *Samuel Johnson.* New York: Harper & Brothers Publishers, 1878.

STOCKDALE, Percival. *The Memoirs of the Life and Writing of Percival Stockdale, Vol. I.* London: Longman, Hurst, Rees, and Orme, 1809.

STOCKDALE, Percival. *An Elegy on the Death of Dr Johnson's Favourite Cat, with a Note on Dr Johnson's Cats.* New Haven: Yale University Press, 1949.

The Strand Magazine: An Illustrated Monthly, Vol. XXX. London: George Newnes Ltd., 1905.

The Strand Magazine: An Illustrated Monthly, Vol. XLIII. London: George Newnes Ltd., 1912.

SWINHOE, Robert. *Narrative of the North China Campaign of 1860.* London: Smith, Elder, & Company, 1861.

Temple Bar, Vol. CV. London: Richard Bentley & Son, 1895.

TWISS, Horace. *The Public and Private Life of Lord Chancellor Eldon, Vol. III.* London: John Murray, 1846.

TYTLER, Sarah. *The Life of Her Most Gracious Majesty the Queen, Vol. I and II.* Toronto: G. Virtue, 1885.

WALPOLE, Horace. *Horace Walpole and His World, Select Passages from His Letters.* London: Seeley, Jackson, and Halliday, 1884.

WEIR, Harrison William. *Our Cats and All About Them.* Cambridge: The Riverside Press, 1889.

Notes

1. Breton, Guy (1965). *Napoleon and his Ladies*. New York: Coward-McCann Inc., p. 32.
2. Levy, Arthur (1894). *The Private Life of Napoleon. Vol. I*. New York: Scribner and Sons, p. 190.
3. Hall, Henry Foljambe (1901). *Napoleon's Letters to Josephine: 1796–1812*. London: J. M. Dent & Co., p. 15.
4. McLynn, Frank (1997). *Napoleon: A Biography*. New York: Arcade Publishing, p.156.
5. Spence, Joseph. (1820). *Observations, Anecdotes, and Characters of Books and Men*. London: John Murray, p. 38.
6. Twiss, Horace (1846). *The Public and Private Life of Lord Chancellor Eldon, Vol. III*. London: John Murray, p. 272.
7. Ibid., p. 272–273.
8. Ibid., p. 273.
9. Gaskell, Elizabeth (1857). *The Life of Charlotte Brontë, Vol. I*. London: Smith, Elder, and Co., p. 309.
10. Robinson, Agnes Mary Frances (1883). *Emily Brontë*. London: W. H. Allen, p. 108.
11. Gaskell, Vol. I, p. 309.
12. Ibid.
13. *Littell's Living Age, Vol. XIX* (1857). Boston: Littell, Son and Co., p. 410.
14. Gaskell, p. 310.
15. *The Bookman, Vol. XI* (1898). New York: Dodd, Mead, & Co., p. 18. This account was originally printed in the *Free Lance*, 1868 and then reprinted in the *Manchester City News*, 28 December 1896.
16. *The Strand Magazine: An Illustrated Monthly, Vol. XLIII* (1912). London: George Newnes Ltd., p. 691.
17. Merrill, Arthur Lawrence (1901). *Life and Times of Queen Victoria Containing a Full Account of the Most Illustrious Reign of Any Sovereign in the History of the World*. Philadelphia: World Bible House, p. 270.
18. *Bedfordshire Times and Independent* (Bedfordshire, England), 5 July 1860; p. 1. ©The British Library Board.
19. *The Dog Fancier, Vols. 28–28* (Battle Creek: U.S.A.), January 1918; p. 19.
20. *Yorkshire Post and Leeds Intelligencer* (West Yorkshire, England), 10 October 1888; p. 5. ©The British Library Board.
21. Ibid.
22. Ibid.
23. *Hull Daily Mail* (East Riding of Yorkshire, England), 13 November 1888; p. 3. ©The British Library Board.

24. *Some Scarborough Faces Past and Present* (1901). Scarborough: Scarborough Gazette Printing and Publishing, p. 237.

25. Knox, Thomas Wallace (1887). *Dog Stories and Dog Lore.* New York: Cassell & Co., p. 122.

26. *Northern Whig* (Antrim, Northern Ireland). 28 December 1858; p. 4. ©The British Library Board.

27. *Leeds Times* (West Yorkshire, England). 12 March 1887; p. 6. ©The British Library Board.

28. Stephen, Leslie (1878). *Samuel Johnson.* New York: Harper & Brothers Publishers, p. 149.

29. Piozzi, Hester Lynch (1788). *Letters to and from the late Samuel Johnson, LL.D, Vol. II.* London: A. Strahan and T. Cadell, p. 328.

30. Stephen, Leslie, p. 149.

31. Boswell, James (1791). *The Life of Samuel Johnson.* London: J. M. Dent & Sons, p. 392.

32. *Pearson's Magazine, Vol. 5* (1898). London: C. Arthur Pearson Ltd., p. 526.

33. *Harper's Weekly, Vol. 15* (1871). New York: Living History Incorporated, p. 772.

34. Weir, Harrison William (1889). *Our Cats and All About Them.* Cambridge: The Riverside Press, p. 4.

35. *Chatterbox* (1872). London: W. W. Gardner, p. 386.

36. Ibid.

37. *Aberdeen Press and Journal* (Aberdeenshire, Scotland), 29 September 1886; p. 6. ©The British Library Board.

38. *Birmingham Daily Post* (West Midlands, England), 27 September 1886; p. 5. ©The British Library Board.

39. Boyle, Frederick (1879). *Memoirs of Thomas Dodd, William Upcott, and George Stubbs, R.A.* Liverpool: Joseph Mayer, p 31.

40. Ibid.

41. Ibid.

42. *Edinburgh Evening Courant* (Midlothian, Scotland), 2 August 1828; p. 2. ©The British Library Board.

43. *London Evening Standard* (London, England), 20 July 1828; p. 2. ©The British Library Board.

44. *Edinburgh Evening Courant*, p. 2.

45. *Morning Chronicle* (London, England). 16 August 1828; p. 3. ©The British Library Board.

46. *North Devon Gazette* (Devon, England), 4 March 1856; p. 4. ©The British Library Board.

47. Ibid.

48. *Dunstable Chronicle, and Advertiser for Beds, Bucks & Herts.* (Bedfordshire, England), 1 March 1856; p. 4. ©The British Library Board.

49. *St. James's Gazette* (London, England), 1 September 1890; p.7. ©The British Library Board.

50. *Belfast News-Letter* (Antrim, Northern Ireland), 28 August 1894; p. 6. ©The British Library Board.

51. *The Cornhill Magazine, Vol. X* (1864). London: Smith, Elder, & Co., p. 177.

52. *The Gardens and Menagerie of the Zoological Society Delineated, Vol. 2* (1831). Chiswick: John Sharpe, p. 45.

53. Delano, Amasa (1817). *A Narrative of Voyages and Travels in the Northern and Southern Hemispheres.* Boston: E. G. House, p. 442.

54. *The Magazine of Natural History and Journal of Zoology, Botany, Mineralogy, Geology, and Meteorology, Vol. VI* (1833). London: Longman, Rees, Orme, Brown, Green, and Longman, p. 140.

55. *The Portfolio, Vol. IV* (1825). London: William Charlton Wright, p. 162.

56. *The Minerva, Or: Literary, Entertaining, and Scientific Journal, Vol. 1* (1824). New York: J. Seymour Press, p. 364.

57. Keim, Albert and Louis Lumet (1914). *Charles Dickens.* New York: Frederick A. Stokes Company, p. 128.

58. Forster, John (1872). *The Life of Charles Dickens, Vol. I.* London: Chapman & Hall, p. 211.

59. Dickens, Charles (1849). *Barnaby Rudge: A Tale of the Riots of 'Eighty.* London: Chapman and Hall, p. i.

60. Ibid., p. ii.

61. Ibid., p. i.

62. *Whitby Gazette,* (North Yorkshire, England), 16 August 1879; p. 2. ©The British Library Board.

63. Burns, Robert (1859). *The Poetical Works and Letters of Robert Burns.* Edinburgh: Gall & Inglis, p. ix.

64. Chambers, Robert (1856). *The Life and Works of Robert Burns, Vol. II.* Edinburgh: W. R. Chambers, p. 147.

65. Burns, p. ix.

66. *The Literary Gazette and Journal of Belles Lettres, Arts, Sciences, no. 102–153* (1819). London: H. Colburn, p. 252.

67. *Pall Mall Gazette* (London, England), 16 January 1895; p. 3. ©The British Library Board.

68. *Manchester Courier and Lancashire General Advertiser* (Greater Manchester, England), 25 April 1885; p. 9. ©The British Library Board.

69. Birch, George Henry (1903). *London on Thames in Bygone Days.* London: Seeley & Co., p. 87.

70. *Kendal Mercury* (Cumbria, England), 23 April 1870; p. 3. ©The British Library Board.

71. *Ballymena Observer* (Antrim, Northern Ireland), 3 September 1887; p. 9. ©The British Library Board.

72. *Gloucester Citizen* (Gloucestershire, England), 26 August 1887; p. 3. ©The British Library Board.

73. Frikell, Wiljalba (1876). *Magic No Mystery.* London: J. Ogden and Co., p. 328.

74. Ibid., p. 329.

Index